Unseal Your Gratitude

POEMS THAT ILLUMINATE THE BEAUTY IN LIFE

Compiled by **Lauren Brill /The Unsealed**
Contributing Writers:

Kalianah, Aiša Mrkulić, Mercedes Wright, Mallory Lemieux, Marissa Maddox, Cierra Williams, Louise Puma, Ala, Gie Santana, Anissa Alves, Kristen Moxley, Afton Villanueva, Christina Mitma Momono, Shalisa Monique, Rayven Washington, Jake April, Tracy Barnes, Lillian Gardner, Anastasia Grieff, Kaileia Suvannamaccha, Tiara Smith, Cait, Morgan Bland, Jessica Ireland, Catherine Burford, Hannah Gray, Ricardo Castor, La'Tiffany Rasmine, Darlene Cervantes, Amber Shatto, Bailey Gausling, Michelle Ruby, Tatyana Roscoe, Clementine Pallanca, Jonathan Odle, Arela Williams, Soriah McClendon, Taylor Rose, Krystana Mayers, Justina Madelaine, Brianna Rund Gange, Ashelyn Knight, Tasha Uliano, Camille Morris, Alexis Bixler, Victoria Dell'Elmo, Sofia Armstrong, Antoinette Gonzalez, Roxanne De Guzman, Juan Carrillo, Kiera Baity, Dee Hainsworth, Lorie Simonian, Jamell Crouthers, Danette Byatt, Lorinda Boyer, Harley Schechter, Ashleigh Ogg, Olivia Droddy, Jazmine Greene, Jessica Conner, Chloe Mayer, Kiore, Gerald Washington, Maggie Faye, Devananda Vargas, Aimee Concepcion, Jameela Dompier, Mary Freeman, Nicholas Grogan, Mira Catlin, Emily Elder, Rebecca Engle, Tamara Gallagher, Hannah Gonneville, Ray Whitaker, Vicky Rosas, Rick Writes, Rashan Speller, Oswald Perez, Sydney Stablein, Latasha T. Collins, Kebe Chet, Obincent Cineus, Karissa Howden, Maria Colon-Gonzalez, Vision W., Zalma, Anita, Williams, Michelle Julian, Ricardo Albertorio, Mel Taul

Copyright © 2024 by Lauren Brill Media LLC
All rights reserved.

No part of this publication may be reproduced, distributed, or transmitted in any form or by any means, including photocopying, recording, or other electronic or mechanical methods, without the prior written permission of the publisher, except as permitted by U.S. copyright law. However, contributors maintain ownership rights of their individual poems and as such retain all rights to publish and republish their work.

Book Cover by Marija Džafo
Layout Design by Larissa Fleury

2024

ISBN Paperback: 979-8-9888582-9-4
ISBN Ebook: 979-8-9904346-0-8

CONTENT GUIDANCE:
This book contains adult language and content that may be triggering for some. Please read with care.

What is The Unsealed?

The Unsealed (**theunsealed.com**) is a writing community where people write, share, and respond to personal and inspirational open letters. We hold weekly events and conversations, inviting interesting guests to talk to our community about their stories. Our platform aims to heal, empower, connect, encourage, and inspire people to persevere through their problems.

All the stories and poems in this book are written by members of The Unsealed community. Our writers are people of various backgrounds, ages, and writing levels.

If you would like to message someone in this book or read more of their writing, you can plug their username into this url: https://theunsealed.com/members/username/

Index

Introduction – **Lauren Brill** 20

WHY ARE YOU GRATEFUL? 24

Words Of Gratuity – **Kalianah** 26
A Thankless Act – **Aiša Mrkulić** 28
Armani's Eternal Love – **Mercedes Wright** 32
Laughter – **Mallory Lemieux** 36
Life, Recovery, And Me – **Marissa Maddox** 38
Grateful for… My… – **Cierra Williams** 44
A Thank You Letter To The Mother Who Never Would Have Accepted Me – **Louise Puma** 46
Just A Week – **Ala** 54
Alien Thanksgiving – **Gie Santana** 58
Look At Us – **Anissa Alves** 62
A Second Chance – **Kristen Moxley** 66
Grateful – **Afton Villanueva** 70
Sunbursts – **Christina Mitma Momono** 72
Drowning On The Surface – **Shalisa Monique** 74
Unsealed Limitations – **Rayven Washington** 76
Why He Chose Me? – **Jake April** 78
Gratitude – **Tracy Barnes** 80
Grateful Recovering Alcoholic – **Lillian Gardner** 82

Breathing Freely – **Anastasia Grieff** 84
For Inspiration – **Kaileia Suvannamaccha** 88
Dear Incomplete Pt.One1 – **Tiara Smith** 92
What If I Wasn't Very Grateful This Year? – **Cait** 96
August 28, 2021 – **Morgan Bland** 102
Grateful for the Gospely – **Jessica Ireland** 104
A Toast – **Catherine Burford** 106
Grateful – **Hannah Gray** 108
Gratitude – **Ricardo Castor** 110
Time – **La'Tiffany Rasmine** 112
Grateful For Mi Familia – **Darlene Cervantes** 116
Gratitude – **Amber Shatto** 118
Simply Grateful – **Bailey Gausling** 120
Growing With Gratitude – **Michelle Ruby** 124
Great-Full – **Tatyana Roscoe** 126
Lucky – **Clementine Pallanca** 128
The Power Of Choice – **Jonathan Odle** 130
Eye Of The Storm – **Arela Williams** 132
Peace That Passes All Understanding – **Soriah McClendon** 136
The Giving Of A Blessed Life – **Taylor Rose** 138
My Chameleon – **Krystana Mayers** 140
Mercury's Sincerity – **Justina Madelaine** 144
Thank You For Keeping My Existence My Beautiful Boy — A poem Dedicated To My Cat – **Brianna Rund Gange** 146
You – **Ashelyn Knight** 148
Being Seen – **Tasha Uliano** 150
Silence – **Camille Morris**. 152

Grateful Memories – **Alexis Bixler**   154
I Am Grateful – **Victoria Dell'Elmo**   156
An Ode To You, My Love – **Sofia Armstrong**   158
Grateful For Motherhood – **Antoinette Gonzalez**   162
Strangers In Passing – **Roxanne De Guzman**   164
Finding Hope After Darkness – **Juan Carrillo**   168
Holiday Highs – **Kiera Baity**   170
Friends In Transience – **Dee Hainsworth**   172
Clarity – **Lorie Simonian**   174
Grateful For Four Things – **Jamell Crouthers**   178
Hand Over Heart – **Danette Byatt**   180
Thank You, Stonewall – **Lorinda Boyer**   182
Losing And Choosing A Sister – **Harley Schechter**   184
Grateful – **Ashleigh Ogg**   186
What I Am Most Grateful For – **Olivia Droddy**   190
Heterosexual Life Partner – **Jazmine Greene**   192
Eileen – **Jessica Conner**   194
Once Lost, Now Found – **Chloe Mayer**   196
Gratitude For Humanity – **Kiore**   198
Being Able To Be Grateful – **Gerald Washington**   204
I Am Grateful For Blue Skies – **Maggie Faye**   206
Letter To A Friend – **Devananda Vargas**   208
11:11 – **Aimee Concepcion**   210
A Gentle Reminder From Friends – **Jameela Dompier**   212
Holding On – **Mary Freeman**   214
Riviera Paradise: A Poem Inspired by my Stepfather on his Last Birthday – **Nicholas Grogan**   216
Blessed With Gratitude – **Mira Catlin**   220

The Ups And Downs Of Family – **Emily Elder**   222
The Journey – **Rebecca Engle**   224
Many Stories That Made Me – **Tamara Gallagher**   226
A Song Of Thanksgiving – **Hannah Gonneville**   234
Morning Exercises – **Ray Whitaker**   236
Grateful For The moments – **Vicky Rosas**   240
Faithful, Thankful, Grateful – **Rick Writes**   242
Elder Stars In The Star – **Rashan Speller**   246
On My Own Two Feet – **Oswald Perez**   248
Reverence – **Sydney Stablein**   250
I Am Grateful – **Latasha T. Collins**   252
Gratitude – **Kebe Chet**   254
Opportunity And Change Harmonizing With Attitude Of Gratitude – **Obincent Cineus**   256
Simple Gratitude – **Karissa Howden**   258
Transformation – **Maria Colon-Gonzalez**   260
Mi Beautiful Musician – **Vision W.**   264
Grateful – **Zalma**   266
A Truth To Return To – **Anita Williams**   270
To My Ancestory – **Michelle Julian**   272
Gratitude – **Ricardo Albertorio**   274
D. All Of The Above - **Mel Taul**   276

13

Dedication

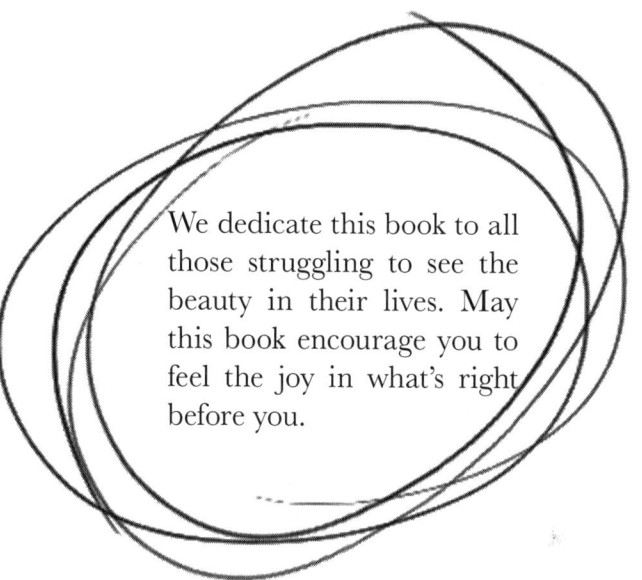

We dedicate this book to all those struggling to see the beauty in their lives. May this book encourage you to feel the joy in what's right before you.

16

UNSEAL YOUR GRATITUDE

POEMS THAT ILLUMINATE THE BEAUTY IN LIFE

18

Introduction

Dear Unsealers,

For a long time, I robbed myself of something I so deserved — something we all deserve. Vividly, I remember being eight years old. The lights were off in my bedroom, and I was supposed to be asleep. Instead, I was crying into my pillow with my dog, Marshmallow, a 20-pound white bichon, at my feet. Frustrated and upset, when I heard my mother walk past my room, I called her to come inside and console me. Immediately, she asked what was wrong.

Completely serious, I looked her in the eye, wiped my tears, and told her, "Mom, I feel like I am not getting anywhere in my career."

My mother gave me a puzzled look and said, "Your career? What career? You're eight! Just be eight."

I thought, "What do you mean just be eight?"

I felt as though she didn't understand me at all. At the time, I dreamed of being an actress and wanted to lay the bricks for my future immediately. The tears I cried at eight returned many times as I spent much of my childhood and young adulthood eager, hungry, and stressed about what was ahead of me.

As a middle schooler, I worried about what college would or would not accept me. By the time I was in high school, I had decided I wanted to be a sportscaster — not an actress — and I constantly thought about where and when I would get my first on-air job. Once I received that dream job after college, I incessantly thought about how to jump to a bigger television market or a better opportunity.

Don't get me wrong; harboring a little ambition is not bad. But I was obsessed with what would be and ignored what was before me.

At eight, I had a picture-perfect, carefree childhood with two loving parents and a brother I greatly admired. My mom packed me peanut butter and jelly sandwiches for lunch, and I beat all the boys at sports during recess (or at least that's how I remember it).

By high school, I had an active social life. I excelled in school and had a ton of support to pursue any and every interest.

When I started working in sports, I had the insane privilege of interviewing legends like Michael Jordan, LeBron James, and Billie Jean King. Heck, I even met Muhammad Ali. While he couldn't speak because of Parkinson's, he pretended to spar with me. Without saying a word, he was charismatic and vibrant.

I had so many incredible experiences. Not to mention, my personal life was filled with tremendous amounts of love.

However, I was so consumed with thinking about what I didn't have or what I ultimately wanted that I never noticed that life was good. Life was very good.

In this book are the submissions from a prompt I gave all of you on TheUnsealed.com. I asked all of you to write about what you are most grateful for in life. I did so because I wanted all of you to give yourselves — maybe even each other — what I stole from myself for way too long. And that is the joy of the present moment.

With immense gratitude,
Lauren Brill

23

WHY ARE YOU GRATEFUL?

By Kalianah
Username: kalianah

Words Of Gratuity

What am I grateful for?
There's a lot you see
I'm not the same girl in the mirror that I see
I'm grateful that my past doesn't define me
Rather, I'm grateful that it has certainly shaped me
I'm so grateful that I'm not as gullible as I used to be
I can read people now, like I can with a book
So that I can finally be free
Free from the toxicity that used to capture me
I am grateful for those around me now
I am surrounded by love that's so loud that it resounds
I no longer worry of what they think of me
I am no longer bound by people pleasing
One of the things I am grateful for,

Is the realization that my life is mine to live and to adore
I can finally be myself without a care in the world
Having that freedom is literally a dream come true
I feel like Boo in the factory of doors,
All of these opportunities that are flying around me
Like they have wings that are so majestic when they soar
I never experienced anything like this
This makes me feel so free
My mind is finally clear
I can focus on bettering me
I am grateful that I still have my drive
No longer procrastinating tasks because of fear
Fear of failure giving people the opportunity to abandon me
I have no fear now because I have real ones beside me.
I am really grateful for my job,
Although it's not where I want to be
I work hard and earn the money that I need to be free
I can buy simple luxuries that make me feel like a queen
I am grateful for the little things like being able to eat and a warm bed.
But as you can see, I wanted to go a little deep
I will leave you with this
My sincerest words
My Words Of Gratuity

Kalianah

By Aiša Mrkulić
Username: aisatheauthor

A Thankless Act

A Thankless Act

I contemplate—
in a grateful state—
where to give thanks.

And it's not long before
little me
is all I can hear and see.

Bursting with glee,
she decrees:

Wendy and Peter Pan,
Neverland,

those who lend a helping hand,
those not afraid
to take a stand.

Pen in hand,
flow-state
is where I land—
filled with child-liked wonder,
and free of fears I've shunned her.

A poem—
this poem—

slowly begins to take its form.
Its words are ones of warmth
that lull her,
hug her—
keep her safe from all-the-world's thunder.

And it's reading
better than planned.

But in truth,
I'm grateful for it all—
the planned and unplanned.

For every version of me
I've met firsthand.

Me when I'm mad,
but what I really am is sad.

Me when I'm glad
that someone tried to understand

rather than write me off
as "bad."

The ability to feel—
a chance to heal
and give to myself
the gift of being real.

Grateful,

for the voice inside my head—
the one I used to dread.

Oh, we'd go head-to-head.
And if you asked my heart
to tell you the worst part,

it'd say
that there was nowhere to hide.

Hard to believe that nowadays,
that voice is on my side.
So, I'm happy-er inside.

Because grateful is what I am
for the will to survive,
thrive,
and come alive

that it's instilled in 'we'.

Today,
it supports the best version of me—
wants for me to get ahead,
does things like remind me when it's time for bed.

Swoops in on a rope
when I'm short on hope,
when I'm hanging by a thread.

But most of all…

what I'm most grateful for…
is every decision
I can call mine—
those made by me
and me
Alone.

The ones I own.

For to them,
I owe this home—
the home
that is
she.

The only place I'm truly, finally
free.

Aiša

By Mercedes Wright
Username: mercedes3650

Armani's Eternal Love

I will never forget the day I had four different doctors tell me that there would be no chance of me ever having a healthy pregnancy and a safe delivery. The outpour of emotions I felt made all the color leave my body and I sat still in silence for a moment without ever responding to the doctors. More than anything in the world, I always wanted to become a mom. I was born with a nurturing spirit. Growing up as a little girl at the age of just two years old I took on the responsibilities of taking care of my younger sister, Armani, who was diagnosed with a rare genetic disorder called metachromatic leukodystrophy. It causes a loss of motor skills, muscle functions and memory. I learned how to feed my sister, change her medicine tubes, and keep her clean. Honestly, from what I remember it never felt like a job to me. I just enjoyed being able to spend time with my sister and making her happy. I was grateful to have her and I always cherished our time together. Unfortunately, with this disorder her life expectancy was cut short. At the age of five years old she took her last breath in my father's arms. I prayed that one day I could become a loving mother and take care of my daughter the way I nurtured my sister. My health was declining significantly and the amount of stress I endured on a day-to-day basis was leading me down a path to destruction. I prayed constantly and asked God to guide me, to please take over. I didn't have any fight left in me to bear any more harm to myself. God spoke to me and reassured me that I will become what I was destined to be if I was willing to sacrifice and start all over: Give up unhealthy eating habits, toxic people in my life, and looking for love in all the wrong places.

I began writing in my journal more often and just about every day I wrote at least one thing I'm grateful for to express my gratitude. Changing my perspective on life and letting go of all that no longer served me, elevated my life tremendously. I had no particular timing in mind. I was focused on the "win" and not "when" all that was promised to me would happen. I was grateful to be on the right track and getting back to me. Redefining my self worth and understanding what it means to love myself just as I am and how to be a better me. Yet, six months later I met the love of my life not knowing he would be more than I could ever imagine in a partner. My best friend, teammate, lover, and protector. We developed our relationship with peace, love, and understanding. During this time, my partner also respected and supported my healthy lifestyle and did everything in his power to ensure I was at my best. After a year of being together, we got the greatest surprise on his birthday. I was pregnant! We were so overjoyed and nervous all at once. As soon as we found out, I immediately thought about what all those doctors told me and I decided to erase that from my mind and speak life, peace, and love into my pregnancy. On March 13, 2022 I gave birth to my beautiful healthy baby girl Armani. We both decided to name our daughter after my sister. My daughter has her own personal angel watching over her. Life has truly shown me that even in times of strife, to always be grateful. You never know what's waiting for you on the other side of the storm.

Mercedes Wright

By Mallory Lemieux
Username: wordsmatter

Laughter

The sun sets and my heart floods
Colors of reds purples and blues
It breaks for the broken
And celebrates for the joyous
As I unwind from the deluge of the day

Little squeals of delight
echo from bedrooms down the hall
Pitter patter of feet
Carry loud laughter of little boys
into the living room where I sit

Laughter;
It's a cashmere sweater cradling a broken heart

And for a moment it turns shoulder rocks into feathers
It's a glimpse of light lessening the dark

It can be heard amongst happiness
And even grief.
Memories and regrets
Reminding us of the duality of the human experience

Without laughter, I could not endure this shattered world
So It is laughter for which I am grateful.

Mallory

By Marissa Maddox
Username: marissamaddox

Life, Recovery, And Me

The thing I am most grateful for in life
is life itself
my life. this life. me.
this may seem obvious, mundane, oversimplified
but not for me
I have anxiety,
depression,
complex PTSD *(post-traumatic stress disorder)*,
and BPD *(Borderline personality disorder)*
I always sort of shrugged at the anxiety;
worry is my natural state
and it always has been
it's all I've ever known
but the depression, the PTSD, the BPD-

those came with time and unfortunate circumstances
the way they blend together and feed off of each other;
the fight is three against one and seems unfair

The little me in the photographs
she stares back at me so innocently
so timid and scared, so wholesome
she has no idea about all of the trauma that's coming her way
she is going to face abuse and neglect
every day for the next couple of decades
and this will shape her forever
I am grateful for this version of myself
because she got me through the hardest time of my life
I talk about her in the third person
because I never felt connected to past versions of myself
but especially the littlest version
I had to cope with too much back then;
I repressed so much of it
now I can't remember huge chunks of my life
but they were too painful to experience the first time around
without having to carry the burden of memory, too

I neglected myself for most of my life,
never stopping to ask what I wanted or needed,
only concerned with pleasing others so I could survive
my default setting was a blank slate
ready to be molded into whatever the other person expected
from me

this was conditioned in me
I was groomed to be the perfect victim
for anyone who wanted to control someone else;
a plague that would follow me well into my adult years
ignoring myself became so normal that I forgot who I am,
or maybe I never knew at all,
I was never given the space to find out
(hence the BPD)

I looked death in the eyes that summer
depression dared me to
BPD agreed
PTSD instigated
and I gave in
they convinced me that my life is worthless
and that I am a burden
how are they so good at that?
the overdose felt like a slow death
eventually I passed out
I don't know how long I was unconscious for
definitely hours, maybe days
when I woke up and realized I was still alive
I was fucking pissed
I was immediately prepared to try again
I can't really explain exactly what changed, or when, or why
recovery was a slow, excruciating process that I didn't want
to participate in
I guess I learned how to participate anyways

little by little, one step at a time
and the pain started to feel a little less intense, a little less often
so to be able to say today that I am grateful for this life
it is an accomplishment,
one that only came after a long and gruesome
recovery process

I am grateful for the version of myself
that packed up all of my things
and moved out of my toxic environment
not once, not twice, but three times
in order to save myself
I am grateful for the version of me
that went to therapy for six years;
the version that took the time
to stare at all of my trauma,
find its roots,
and pour love into them
the way I always deserved
I unlearned a lifetime of self-hatred
and as a 23-year-old woman
I began to learn how to take care of myself
and maybe even grow to love myself

It has been a long, tiresome journey to this place of gratitude
I could never see a future for myself before
but now I'm starting to
so this is what I mean when I say I am grateful for my life

and I am grateful for myself
I'm grateful for all the different versions of me
that had to exist in order to carry me through
a lifetime of trauma and neglect
I got myself through everything
the world had to throw at me
without ever letting it take away my softness
or my hope for the possibility of something better
the fact that I am alive today is a privilege
and that is what I am most grateful for
I am grateful to simply be alive and to be me

Marissa Maddox

By Cierra Williams

———————

Grateful For... My...

My present is not a reflection of my pass
As a homeless child... I missed out on a lot
I remember eating beans and rice out of that small black pot
The cuddling next to my mother and two brothers just to get heat... never complaining because I was told there were other kids who wished they had food to eat.
Sleeping on the floor of someone else's house
Feeling lucky if they had a couch.
A part of me always wondered why it was so hard for us to get our own and finally after years we had a place to call home.
Some would ask what I'm grateful for in life
From most women you'd hear, to be a mother, have a family, and become a wife... But me I'm grateful for life lessons
The ones that cause you to struggle but are secretly a blessing

The ones that teach value
That shield your name from the mouths of people
you've outgrown
So what am I grateful for in life you ask
Walking out the grocery store with food even if it means
going up 18 stairs with heavy bags
I'm grateful for the gas that equates to heat... so I can cook
up some meat
I'm grateful for things that the average person takes for granted
I know what it's like to be without it
An experience most will never know but it's moments like
this that allowed me to blossom and grow.
What am I grateful for you ask ... that my present is not a
reflection of my past

Cierra Williams

By Louise Puma
Username: louisepuma

A Thank You Letter To The Mother Who Never Would Have Accepted Me

I know on paper I am your least favorable candidate to love your son, let alone marry him
Yet I can promise you, no one will ever love your son the way I did
I am white, with just a Bachelor's degree working in the same medical practice as him
Yet I have studied every eyelash, laugh line, and beauty mark your son has
The way his energetic eyes are laser focused when he is listening to help heal someone else
The way his whole face brightens when he greets his patients
How his laugh fills up every room he is in and how it feels like a big hug to me
I know exactly where he is most ticklish and where to hold him when he needs support

I am not a part of your culture, I don't speak your language
and I am not religious
Yet, I worshiped and adored the ground your son walked on
and not because an ancient holy text told me to but because
I saw the way he worked miracles every day
Even and especially on his worst days
How he cared for people so deeply and fully and taught me
to do the same

I have so many unanswered questions for you
When was the first time he made you proud?
When was the first time he made you really angry?
Does his mischievous side, while driving you crazy, also help
keep life exciting like it always did for me?
Who does he get his big, lively, beautiful, wondrous brown
eyes from?
And does it warm your soul to see the way they widen when
he speaks about something he's passionate about?
And that he only ever gets angry on behalf of others and
those less fortunate than him?
Did the first time you saw him cry make your whole body
stiffen and realize just how much you really love him?
And that you would do anything to protect him from any
kind of hurt? Even if it meant hurting yourself?
Did the first time you heard his laugh melt your heart
like butter?
And make you wonder how you went your whole life and
just now finding the most perfect sound?
Did it make you a lighter person because nothing feels as
good as laughing with him?

Does it make you proud that he never lost that childish sense of humor?
How does it feel to know you created my favorite sound?
How does it feel to know you made my favorite everything in human form?

I don't speak your language, celebrate the same religious holidays, or have the same lived experiences as you due to the difference in our skin tones
Yet, I share so much of your son's values that we swore we were soulmates

Our strong sense of family — how much we are both loved by family and how important it is to return that love
To remain idealistic and hopeful despite the difficulties of the world
Our ability to laugh nonstop at the same inside joke for 10 minutes that we cannot even look at each other without another bout of laughter powering through
Having felt the darkest depths of human emotion possible making us strive to be better humans every day and to service others
To be a good person even and especially when no one is looking
That the person you think you have nothing to learn from, actually may have the most valuable wisdom
Being hopelessly indecisive yet still being sure we were in healthcare as a life calling for a reason — and we were meant to meet to each other
That nothing felt as good as when we first laid eyes on each other and saw the other person's whole face light up

The naughty risk of eating chips and salsa in white bedding
Yearning for the simplest dream of having each other to come home to and take the day off with, to make a home within each other
How could such a simple dream be so forbidden?

We were both so fucking cruelly lucky and unlucky at the same time to have befriended each other and then fall deeply in love
At first a slow burn from colleague, to friendship, to companionship to falling deeply in love
Like a head on collision
We saw it coming but neither of us knew how to stop it or wanted to
I'll never love someone as wholly and unconditionally as I love him — yes, in present tense

My world shattered when I laid in the same bed as him, the same bed we had just made love in and he said "you're just not part of my world"

I instinctively grabbed his hand and we just laid there in silence
Looking at the same ceiling, laying in the same sheets
Hearing the same buzz of the city outside and feeling the same coolness from the window being propped open
We were both covered in goosebumps, our palm sweat was seeping into each other's skin
My heart was pounding because I knew what he said was the truth

And he knew how painful it was for me to hear and he could never take it back
Because it was true
I was not a part of his world

It didn't matter that every countertop, nightstand, and mirror was littered with sticky notes of affectionate reminders of how much I adored him
Or that his fridge was full of healthy snacks and ice cream I had bought him
Or that he always had my favorite shirt of his, with all the beaches of Brazil, cleaned and the first shirt in his pajama drawer for me to run in and change into as soon as we were home for the night
Or that the steamer he uses every day for his scrubs I got him
Or his favorite letter I ever wrote him which was one from Trader Joe's and had the quote "You can't stop the waves but you can learn to surf" lay in his nightstand underneath his "The Holy Geeta"
Or all the hopes and dreams and laughs and tears and more laughs and more hugging and embracing that we had
Nothing would change that I was not a part of his world

To you, I may have never been enough
Not educated enough
Not religious enough
Not cultured enough
Not well traveled enough
But I can promise you one thing, I loved your son with every fiber of my being
And I painstakingly always will

Even as he was telling me how it could never be me I was
praying and illustrating the woman who it would be
Because as heartbroken as I am the only thing more
unimaginable is him never being fully happy and still
being alone

He's the cause of my biggest heartbreak, but he's also one of
the best things that ever happened to me
I am a fundamentally changed and better woman because I
knew and loved him
I still pray for him every day
I pray he finds his happiness and peace

More than anything else, I want to thank you
Thank you for choosing to bring him into this world, so
if nothing else, even the chance of loving him was made
possible because of you
I'll never know you; but you made my favorite person
And that's an even sadder love story
That despite this heartache I carry every day, I'll never be
able to explain to you how grateful I am for him
How lucky I felt to know and love him

And even more than creating my favorite person
Being heartbroken by him has made me even more
enamored with my own father
Who never told me who, what or why I had to pick
a certain path
Who refused to see me cry, not because he felt I was too
weak but because he refused to see his little hopeful, loving,
unafraid girl be beaten down by this world

Who even as he saw me break apart to love your son,
still had empathy for him because he, as a father, could
not imagine telling his own children to walk away from
someone who truly loved them just because they're from a
different culture
Thank you for reminding me how lucky I am to have a
father who makes me feel exquisitely seen

Louise

By Ala
Username: ala

Just A Week

Tomorrow marks 2 years since you left
breaking the entirety of my being in ways I didn't know were possible.

but, I'm not sad anymore.

I can finally say your name without trembling
and my heart doesn't skip a beat anymore when I think about you.
Don't take this wrong and think that I don't still love you because I do,
I always will
and nothing can change that.

because E.,
in the years since our eclipse,
no one has ever come close to
making me feel
as loved and accepted as you.
not even myself.

you changed me
and I am sincerely better for it.
the eternal gift of your love and for this I will always
be grateful.

self-ideation was a just a concept and
I had no idea who I was before you
showed me what it felt like to be
received with intention.

I will never forget your smile
the first night we met
or how gently we kissed in front of Rebar
listening to my favorite band on repeat.
("one more hour" was always my favorite track, but now it's
even more special because of you.)

I never got the chance to tell you but E,
you quite literally launched me into this new life as a poet
and propelled my devotion to spirituality.
that one rose quartz caused it all and now I have more
crystals than I can even count

every time I get a new one, I think of you
and I've finally stopped favoring ones that are blue.
I've most recently started gravitating to purples and pinks.
a symbolic representation of my journey of trying to fall in
love after you.

I've had to learn the hard way that no one will ever love me
like you did
and I'm not saying that out of pity or remorse at all.
It just makes what we shared all the better because you are
the blueprint
You made falling in love feel like a dream.
You are the reason I know to never settle
and know what it means to reach perfection because you
saw it in me
and nurtured it even when you knew you'd have to leave.

That used to make me sad but I understand why now.

Without your influence, I would be doing so much worse.
I definitely would have settled
and probably gotten stuck with a baby
co-created by someone not even worthy of my energy.
(SINCERELY...THANK YOU!!!!)

I've written so much about you and I don't think I'll ever stop.
A part of me will always miss you
but I know that we weren't meant to be
A forbidden love

with a man lost at sea.
My literal sailor and hero
in the U.S Marines

Thank you for gracing me with your presence.
Thank you for seeing what I didn't know existed inside of me.
Thank you for teaching me that feeling and connection are
not something to fear.
Thank you for showing me the importance of surrendering
to the universe,
to trust the process and just flow.
Thank you for making me a poet
and forcing me to grow and
receive new love in ways
I never even dreamed

You really did change me E.
and for that, I will always be grateful.
I don't know if you'll ever see this,
but that won't stop me from giving flowers when they are
due and my one regret is not being able to give you that
while you were still here.
So E.
if this does ever find you,
all I really wanna say is
thank you <3

Ala <3

By Gie Santana
Username: giesantana

Alien Thanksgiving

I am grateful for the tear-stained letter full of encouragement and conviction that ending my life in 2019 would have been better, landed on the ears of a mighty God.

I am grateful that the strength I gave others, i.e.; church mothers, displaced lovers, friends and even animals of the forest, finally showed up for me.

It held my four-leaf clover. I got lucky. I guess my life really wasn't over.

Strength, I am grateful for you, you're one clever lover.

It wasn't my time. I keep saying over and over.

THIS time though, it IS.

Time to accelerate life and honor every one of those wishes.
The ones that were blown from candles perched atop a thick slice of chocolate cake.
Nestled on a paper plate because who wanted to do dishes?

It's time to collect from the wells where I tossed many a shiny penny, sometimes dimes too because everybody knows those wishes count as double and I really need them to come true.

It's time to give myself the grace that I have granted so many.

Grateful for an anchor of a soul that rests deep within a 9 year old.
At 9 years old, He saved the souls of plenty.

Next of kin, grateful for unwavering love from a Mother whose heart is worn with worry. But she is a warrior, a protector.
A galaxy of love wrapped prayers is what I am grateful for.

Grateful for loss.
It hurts so bad at first. But the loss can be a gain with unseen wings, I now am finally starting to feel like myself again.

Grateful for the grit.
Without it, there's so much I wouldn't have been able to accomplish.

Not even half of it.

Grateful that I am choosing to love myself more, and the self love I poured in is opening all sorts of new doors.

In the hallways of life, I am grateful.

For the heartfelt wrongs and the astonishing rights, for the affirmations I recite before bed each night, the nourishing food that illuminates my soul like a light, the emotions I wear on my sleeve so those around me can see the real me…
I am grateful.

For everything on this planet will be alright.

Nano-Nanooo, Gie

By Anissa Alves
Username: poeticbounce

Look At Us

Wow, look at us
1,095 days later
In a space we never thought we'd be in
But look at us
We are happy
Smiling ear to ear
Full of so much joy
Full of so much thanks
The sun never shined so bright
Remember when we hated ourselves so much
We couldn't stand to look at ourselves in the mirror
Wanting to give up but knowing we couldn't
Feeling like we were letting ourselves down
For every day we let pass not pouring into us and our needs

Every day waking up not knowing where we would
be mentally
Every journal entry we wrote for the last three years
All we wanted to do was grow
All we wanted was to be free
Free from the feelings of life weighing down on us so heavy
Living wasn't fun anymore

Look at us we made it
We broke free from the feelings of disappointment of self
For hurting someone we love so much
We'd walk across the ocean and back
No questions asked
There is nothing on this earth we wouldn't do
We felt so much shame
We felt so much guilt
We felt so much hurt
For breaking down the one person who held us up
When everyone else let us down
We carried the burden of it all but not anymore

Look at us
No more guilt
No more shame
No more self-doubt
No more self-sabotage
We worked so hard for this
So many sleepless nights
So many tears that were cried
For us to be right here in this moment
We stepped into this year knowing it was ours

Our year to be grateful
Grateful for every step in our journey
Our year to be proud of how far we've come
We told ourselves we weren't leaving this year without
our degree
We kept our promise
We made it happen
That fight was hard
A fight we were ready to give up on
We were so close we could taste it
So we made sure to push through

Look at us
We navigated through self-sabotage
We navigated through the feelings of not feeling enough
Losing confidence in ourself
Almost forgetting who we were
Feeling like we couldn't get through the storm
Feeling like the light at the end of the tunnel was one that
was too far
Feelings of knowing we were our worst enemy
Trapped with the fears of letting go
Having to let go of habits that provided us comfort for all
these years
We had to let them go one by one
We are still on the journey of shedding habits that no longer
serve us
All while appreciating the ones that are no longer here

Look at us, we made it
Every day we wake up grateful

Grateful for every tear that was shed
Every low that was felt
Every moment we spent alone praying to be exactly where we are
1,095 days ago this space seemed as distant as the moon is from earth
But I am grateful
Grateful to have had you along with me
Riding this ride to this place where we can say we are finally free

Poetic Bounce

By Kristen Moxley
Username: lunchboxmoxx

A Second Chance

In the morning, I kneel and pray
Thankful for another day
To be alive and wonder aloud
Because today I can be proud

A selfish thing once was I
Drinking and using, living a lie
Now I am free from burden and strife
I'm grateful that I can live my life

I'm grateful for another chance
To exist in this world, to steal a glance
At what my future could possibly hold

And to see what my story will unfold

Here in the present there are many things
Paintings to paint, and songs to sing
Hands to grasp, and lips to kiss
A life to live, I nearly did miss

I'm grateful for grass underneath my feet
I'm grateful that my heart still beats
I'm grateful that I choose myself
I'm grateful for my growing health

Each day I live brings something new
A different thought, a sky so blue
And with supportive family and friends
I'm grateful that my life won't end

But what I am most grateful for
Is having you walk through my door
A love I cannot ever explain
You are my sun and falling rain

With you by my side, there's always light
Hope and joy and sparks ignite
I'm grateful to be sober with you
And to live a life I never knew

Everything means so much to me

I never thought that I could be
Happy and in a better place
A second chance to show me grace

I'm grateful at night to go to sleep
And dream a dream so very deep
But before all that, I kneel and pray
And thank God for another day

Kristen Moxley

By Afton Villanueva
Username: poeticdiabetic

Grateful

WHAT AM I MOST GRATEFUL FOR?
We Have A Technology Allowing Meaningful Interactions, Making Ourselves Share These Gifted Realities, Also Too, Especially For Unconditionally Loving Families, Our Roots.
What am I most grateful for?
If you've woken up and chose to keep going. Whether you're in the calm seas of peace, or you're riding the lows and highs of the waves that never seem to sleep.
What am I most grateful for?
To be able to create poems that explain the emotions I've grown in a strange dream that dreams to explore and release more. I'm grateful for my eyes, because there was a time in my life where I was legally blind for a week, and I remember thinking "how will I ever see what my drawings

look like?" I'm grateful for the advances in modern medicine, for without it I wouldn't have lasted past a few months without the creation of insulin. I'm grateful I've made it to 14 years past my date of diagnosis, and I plan to keep on going, despite the lows of highs of these waves that never seem to sleep (But always seem to dream). I'm grateful I've been able to come across the unsealed letters that reveal the real miracles that have survived and thrived through all types of weather.
What am I most grateful for?
The family that's handed me a purpose to see the dirt and to keep planting these seeds for you to read and examine, and to hopefully inspire a type of higher connection to yourself to seek the life that you deserve, and to know that each and every one of us are worth way more than worthless.

Afton Villanueva

By Christina Mitma Momono
Username: cmitmamomono

Sunbursts

a little toddler dabbles her toes in the Oregon coast waters,
giggling and running from near her mamas.
her Portland cousins play near here with Auntie creating
castles, jungles and rivers that flow the waves of the
ocean waves and ecovillages below – the land, the sand
interconnected to the depths of deepness below.
the sunbursts softly touch the reunion moments that cannot
occur all the time.
sunbursts.
small joyful stands cheering for their favorite college teams,
swag outfits of hopes to hoops of dreams – we all have
our shots.
for the beats that native musicians drum up to bless, to heal
and to cheer the crowds to love,

the therapist who sits in her own softness after healing,
handing out hope through listening and assisting struggles
of pain, finding laughter and humor to balance out
the darkness.
the sunbursts come through the bubbled grey clouds that
temporarily pop up as life below saunters in shimmers to
only be captured in the seconds that exist.
no tomorrow is promised.
no big kiss, no big hug, no sounds — so soak in it all.
soak in the life that leaves us to grow embedded in mother
earth- pachamama and inti love — quechuan indigenous
circles lift up and offer munay — deep love- — where
sunshine spreads limitlessly.

Christina Mitma Momono

By Shalisa Monique
Username: shalisamoniquespeaks

Drowning On The Surface

My Faith Is Being Tested
The Enemy Wants To Ensure That My Meter Reaches Restless
Oxygen At 100 But I Have A Slight Confession
I'm Drowning On The Surface And I Could Be Gone
In Seconds
I Just Need One Reason To Keep Fighting These Demons
To Make It Through My Season Genie In A Bottle Give
Me Something To Believe In
The Surface Is Uneven And That Hole I Filled Has Steepened
Life Keep Throwing Punches And This Is A Brutal Beating
Life Is What You Make It But There's A Deeper Meaning
End Isn't Final Just Next Step Of Completion
When God Is For You Who Can Be Against You?
Tell Me What's The Issue
Statements Sounding False And The Facts Look Artificial

If I Gave You This Size 7 And I Made It Fit Your Feet
Could You Handle All The Pressure That Comes With
Being Me?
If I Wrote It Step By Step Would You Understand
Directions?
Or Give It What You Got And Just Wait For The Corrections
See I Have To Be Direct Cause I'm Not Good With Rejection
I Had To Bite The Bullet Where's The Love & Affection?
They Told Me Use My Voice To Build Better Connections
But Left Me 6 Feet Under Without Air Or Protection
The Enemy Whispered "Will You Float Or Will You Fall"
I Replied With Grace
"God Is Light; In Him There Is No Darkness At All" 1
John 1:5
My Strength To Shake It Off He Helped Me Walk Before I
Crawled
It's Time To Take A Bow How Bout A Round Of Applause
His Preserving Power Allowed The Force From Within To
Not Just Move Mountains But Forgive Me For My Sins
The Devil Tried To Shake Me, Forgetting He Who Made
Me And I Know This May Sound Crazy But He Does It
On A Daily
Grateful To Be More Than A Name In A World Full Of
Pain Where The Things That Keep Me Sane Are From
Things I Can't Explain
Faith Leads To Victory And I Am On A Mission
Breaking Every Barrier With God As My Witness

Shalisa Monique

By Rayven Washington
Username: rayven_butanyways_prettylady

Unsealed Limitations

Speaking to every fighter
I'm so grateful that GOD took a chance on ME
Thankful that I am his rider
His unconditional love is beyond measures
His unconditional love is so comforting
Tangible and intangible
I just love the way GOD loves me
Don't you see
If giving up was easy
Everyone would have taken a back seat
Including me
I'm grateful for GOD's presence
Most importantly never leaving me
Looking at my reflection

I'm grateful the mirror is always in front of ME
In the presence of darkness
GOD'S love always trembles the unseen
What are the fighters singing
Worthy Worthy Worthy
It's a grateful human being

Rayven Washington

By Jake April
Username: jsapril

Why He Chose Me?

What am I grateful for?
Often I feel shameful for not feeling more grateful for
my disability
I am grateful to the Higher Power
For instilling the motivation and strength
Recognizing how I can use my disability
Sometimes I make myself feel dizzy
Trying to figure out why me
he chose to be looked at differently
I never think I will fully love my disability
Because I do wish my disability wasn't something you can see
But when I look at my life now
I am trying to see something new
The good in why he chose me
Being one of the people whose disability you can see

So you see
There is a responsibility
To encourage others to see
We all have a "disability"
I don't want self-pity
I just want people to understand that
"Your disability" just maybe
Your greatest ability
Thank you Higher Power
And everyone that supports me!

Jake

By Tracy Barnes
Username: poeticaddiction_365

Gratitude

I'm forever grateful
That I am able to share my words
With people
And they often become inspired
By my positivity and willingness to share
Openly and comfortably
Everything I've been through
From heartache to heartbreak
There is no shame
Just lessons to be learned
I'm grateful for them all
Teachable moments that make me stand tall
I practice gratefulness every day
That's why I'm grateful for everyone

I encounter daily
From strangers I meet on the street
To inconnus that have become great supporters
In any and everything I do
I'm forever grateful for restored love
Especially the woman that accepted me
And made me appreciate love again
Thank you for first being a friend
I'm forever grateful
For existing in a world
That doesn't want you to survive
But I find a way to survive the odds stacked against me
Blessed to be alive
And continuously see
That I'm surrounded by the people meant to help me navigate this life!

Tracy Barnes

By Lillian Gardner
Username: divinelylil

Grateful Recovering Alcoholic

When I first started attending Alcoholics Anonymous (AA) meetings, something I heard a lot of people say in their introduction was that they were a grateful alcoholic. I couldn't understand why someone would be grateful to be cursed with this disease. It destroyed my life, my relationships, my will to live. Why on earth would anyone be grateful to go through life with this sickness? It wasn't until I had a relapse that sent me to such a deep rock bottom that I had to fully surrender myself to the program. Once I did so, I started to push myself out of my comfort zone, making friends, showing up consistently to the same meetings, developing a relationship with my higher power and giving my all to the twelve steps. This is when I started to see the promises of the program coming true. My fear of the world, failure, rejection and judgment started to dissipate. My heart started opening up again and it made space for true connection. I learned how to be vulnerable and share the things I held in so deeply with shame in the past. I have developed so much gratitude for this life of recovery. I understand now what it means to be a grateful recovering alcoholic. If I never had this disease I would have never met the beautiful souls I have in my life today. I would have never gone to the depths of my soul and discovered who I truly am underneath all of my fears and pain. I would have never felt the connection of such a powerful, loving and accepting community. AA is my family and I am so grateful to have been led here through my struggles.

Lillian Gardner

By Anastasia Grieff
Username: anastasia_grieff

Breathing Freely

Upon summers conclusion
Life enables transformation,
Forcing temperatures to plummet
Causing leaves to crash down
Sparking tragedy among reality regarding moments,
our sun involuntary shows her face less and less each day
In replacement of enabling
seasonal depression's attempts
to drag my spirit down a path
similar to the leaves,
I perceive it as
a natural exigent
transition in life that
motivates me to analyze reasons

I am eternally grateful to participate in this lifetime
Blessed for every opportunity I receive
allowing me to join the audience as the wind chants,
her whimsical songs while dancing among the trees,
reminds me of being free
Embracing the anxiety,
Obtained from hearing her melody make its way.
Anticipating that moment she manifests the ability to flutter
through me
While attempting to take my hair
for a ride as she passes by,
causing it to freely fly,
leaving behind a feeling of being alive
Embracing times
I can supervise devoted water
rapidly rushing to his designated destination,
Crashing and blasting as he barrels past whatever hinders
the path
While empowering natural flow
I divert my focus down below to the surface
that serves a crucial purpose of
supplying an extraordinary ability called opportunity,
while providing all power to evolve
This almighty surface that gifted us a purpose to
progress consistently for all eternity,
therefore forever i'll idolize this world
and all it's achieved
I shall cherish moments that remind me

what life is supposed to be
worshiping every second
I'm able to explore life's
beautiful natural sense of harmony,
that nature attempts to maintain a mystery
I shall permanently honor
all opportunities, life presents me
most importantly I am immensely grateful
for times
I can simply breathe,
As I sit
listening to the trees
bringing me to feel
free

Anastasia Eliza Grieff

By Kaileia Suvannamaccha
Username: kaithepocketbuddha

For Inspiration

To the songs that soothe our souls—
Birds, who give voice to the dust on butterfly wings,
that set flight to hearts that weigh more, in life,
than this human body can bring

To the women, who hold me in their arms—
Mothers whose love gives birth to all others,
their lips, dripping with truths we crave to read
in the lies of men that can't, who weren't made to, bleed.

To the love rising from the ashes within me,
turning dust to nectar, nourishing
petals that sprout, even through fallen leaves.

To the mind, that relentless dynamo,
that wonders, even as I slumber.

To these hips I haven't mastered
how to shake, that I call home.

To these hardy bones
I fear to break, that I know one day
will wither away.

To these eyes, I know
take me deeper
inside

To the true me, myself, and I,
I've always known.

To the one who reads these words,
a reflection, a shadow

That, beneath a fruit tree
already lived and died
longer than

You, or me,
an extension of interconnection,
sparks that lead us back to one eternal flame
from which we all light, and delight,
in one another.

To the hands that type, these words
into a device that may one day enslave me

To pen and paper that cramps my hand,

an addictive catharsis that gives semblance to

This life, this foreign concept,
a system my brain can't think itself free from,
a headache, a heartache, all at once
felt and embraced,
yet unbound.

For all of this,
I am grateful.

Kaileia

By Tiara Smith
Username: tirasm

Dear Incomplete Pt. One

Dear Self,

It is not often that we take time away from the sometimes uncontrollable spiral that is our life to think about the things that we are grateful for within it.
And, now that I've taken time to think about it, I've come to the realization that most people aren't grateful until they are given a reason to be.
Maybe it's my unhealthy obsessions with psychology and horror speaking, but he wasn't entirely wrong in his thinking.
People who have been in car accidents tend to be more grateful for life than people whose lives have never been threatened.

Maybe that's off-topic.
What am I GRATEFUL for?

I suppose I'm grateful for the interdependence of humans and trees.
People don't really think about small things such as these.
I'm grateful for the way the wind blows through the leaves,
and the way my son hugs me before he leaves.

You know what?

I'm grateful for life. My life. As it is now.

Just last year, my mental health was depleting. My fiancé of seven years was facing several years in prison, and I'd lost my mind along with him. I remember how bad things got.

Moment of silence to a dark past that led to a brighter future.

Maybe I could have shared a story, but I've just been in deep thought. What am I grateful for?

Everything. I remember having nothing like it was yesterday. I remember praying for something to happen any day. I remember hoping that I could find a way. I remember.

So I'm grateful for every breath and every stomach growl. I'm grateful for feeling sick and smelling something foul.

Things that people don't think about. Things that people can't do.

I'm grateful for everything because I remember when I didn't have anything.

Love,
Self

Tiara Allure Smith

By Cait
Username: clmcreatives

What If I Wasn't Very Grateful This Year?

It was hard to be appreciative this year.
It is always hard to appreciate things in life when everything else becomes so heavy.
I think maybe gratitude is just a way to remain hopeful through despair;
to remind us that we should be glad that we even have the opportunity to feel those feelings and have experiences in the first place.

Over the past year I was thankful for a few things;
I was thankful that I got a new job,
that my mom let me move home,
that I am safe and healthy,
and I can confidently say I was and am thankful for my cat.

At the very least, I should probably be thankful that I am
afforded the luxury of being able to not be super grateful.
I suppose every day that I am alive, living and breathing, I
should be glad.

Although, I wasn't the one that chose to be here.
I have to face responsibility that I did not ask for.
Truth be told, I don't even choose to show up every day;
some days I stay in bed and do nothing for myself.
A while ago I just decided that I have to keep myself alive
and learn the lessons of life.

I wish I was more grateful.

Maybe if I was more gracious of the good things, I would
also react better to the negatives.

This year I tried to force myself to be thankful even through
the things that made me most uncomfortable:
the things that made my stomach churn, my heart ache,
and left the corners of my eyes stained red.

I cannot be thankful for all of the negative things; I cannot
be thankful for unkindness, pain, hardship, loss, and grief.
I do not want to find the good in every situation because
sometimes things just suck.
I do not want to appreciate these things because I do not
want to accept them.

Sure I wouldn't feel so sad right now if I was able to trust the process.

How could I be glad that I don't feel strong enough to accomplish any goals or that my family members are spending their nights sinking into depression?
I felt weak a lot.

If I was thankful for every obstacle I have faced, I fear that I might get used to living life in this way.
I don't think I would learn as much.
I need to be uncomfortable.
I need to wonder 'Why me?'

Apparently there is no good or bad way to live-
there are only our feelings, decisions, and lessons we leave with.

I am not grateful for the lessons I learn as I am experiencing them.

A person is not grateful for air when they are being held underwater.
Sure they want to breathe, but it is about the action, not the object.
It is about figuring out how to take a successful breath, and only once a person is back above water, are they thankful for the air itself.

When a person is left underwater panic instills and the individual is only thinking about the fact that they need to get above the water, not about why.

I can't imagine anyone in the middle of a crisis thinking 'Wow I'm so glad to be here.'
So what is one to do when constantly living in a state of dysregulation?

I am suspicious that perhaps I am not finding pleasure or contentment because I am in the midst of one of those big life lessons;
the kind that you look back upon later and see the change it forced you to experience.
Am I supposed to be grateful now for the what's to come later or am I allowed to be sad?
Can I pity the world and still oblige to gratitude and hope?

To be grateful is to express thanks and appreciate the benefits received.
I was not very grateful this year,
but I am thankful that I am able to grow;
grateful that I get to try again.
I am indebted to the world, but I have an obligation to myself.

'She does not have to always be thankful for what has happened because sometimes she knows she deserves more, or at least she's trying to,' I often think.

I don't want to be grateful just because I am told that I have to be.
I don't want the people around me to think that their actions are okay because things can always be worse.
I might be cynical, but I know that life can be a little lighter.
I don't want to be glad with what I do have just because some people have less than me,
I want everyone to have more.

Signed the girl sitting here grateful to be able to express herself (I am still learning how to communicate my gratitude)

Cait

By Morgan Bland
Username: dlamdiva

August 28, 2021

A sweltering Florida night
A room full of twinkling starry lights
The blonde in the little black dress
In a crowd of strangers, looking to impress
A year of joy merged into one
That day my life had just begun
On August 28, 2021

Against all odds standing here
In the face of doubt, mistakes, and fears
Then suddenly my pain made worthwhile
By ocean eyes and a benevolent smile
The one who all the world shunned

In that moment became second to none
On August 28, 2021

Out of that kindness came a vow
To be something greater than I am now
To rise from the doldrums of my malaise
And become worthy of that glowing praise
A promise burns brighter than the sun
And I'll remember until my life is done
That day, August 28, 2021

Morgan

By Jessica Ireland
Username: jireland621

Grateful For The Gospel

I smile and say: "Good morning."
But everyone seems like they are mourning.
Have they not heard the news of our Lord and savior?
Who we will see one day in eternal paradise
He died for our sins upon the cross
Wrongdoing, he committed none.
Rejoice! Be thankful
Our Lord loves us.
He brought me out of darkness
And healed my broken heart
Without him, I would be lost.
Gratitude cannot repay the sacrifices he made.
So I will spread His word until we are united at last.

Jessica N. Ireland

By Catherine Burford
Username: autistkitty

A Toast

A toast to the ones
Who attempted to crush my
Heart of diamonds.

A toast to the one
Who left me hanging without
A single answer.

A toast to the one
Who made me cry for sharing
A giggle or two.

A toast to the one
Who told me to know my place
And left me to drown.

A toast to the one
Who put their reputation
Before a best friend.

A toast to the one
Who loved me up to a point
And not forever.

A toast to the ones
Who've made me the toughest gem
Here on Planet Earth.

Catherine Burford

By Hannah Gray
Username: hgray624

Grateful

Another day of being alive,
searching for the meaning of life,
trapped inside the cage of my mind,
a lost soul breaking free.

Darkness is a friend of mine,
where lost souls go to hide,
so much beauty to be found inside,
open your eyes to see.

Delighted by the somber skies,
melancholy far and wide,
moon peeking over clouds at night,
stars begin to twinkle and shine.

Oh what joy, darkness brings.

Inspiration revealed in the light,
as mother earth comes to life,
cotton candy painted skies,
reflecting off the waterfront.

Brown eyes turn to pools of honey,
golden and bright in the sun,
breathing in the cool fall air,
on a dewy Saturday morning.

Music plays to soothe the soul,
a song for every occasion,
growing through both light and darkness,
for that I am grateful.

h.b.gray

Hannah Gray

By Ricardo Castor
Username:ricky_the_writer

Gratitude

To me life is an ocean you have to keep on swimming to find yours
and love is not only a fortune, it definitely means more

someone keep on pouring oxygen, purpose in our cups
every morning there is a lot of knocking at every door

I am grateful for my family, my friends, the good and the bad and all
to me all of them are stepping stones in life to move on

I am grateful, I will be grateful until I crash and burn
gratitude from yesterday, for today, and for tomorrow…

Ricardo Castor

By La'Tiffany Rasmine
Username: tiffanyj387yahoo-com

Time

It's what I'm grateful for
Along with so much more
For me, time's holding so much in store
So how couldn't I be grateful for (it)?
Without time, I wouldn't have known all of my talents

Time is many second chances when you keep getting off balance
Because the clock keeps ticking
And right there with you while you face the challenges

So grateful for Time
It answers the who's and the whys
Disguises who will stay and who will say goodbye

It wants us to succeed, It gives us so many tries
Which is every reason why

Time was the best thing to come about
Because it's here pushing you until it simply runs out
And then what?
What do you do when that comes about?

That's why Time is here — in your face, in your ears

Time, it screams
Time, it shouts
Begging us to share all our gifts with the world

To help our inner little boy
To help our inner little girl
Time will give him a hug
And safely give her her pearls

Time gives you what you deserve
Time is spacy, Time is curves
Time can get on our nerves
Because we'd rather control it instead of be patient on what it will give us in return

Time is forgiveness
Time is laughter
Time is sadness

But Time is there to get it right again with gladness
Thankful for Time because it's tough and can't be taken for granted

Time will eventually grow all of your seeds, if watered and planted…

La'Tiffany Rasmine

By Darlene Cervantes
Username: darleenc5

Grateful For Mi Familia

Grateful for the lucha, the battle belonging to
the dreamers,
the underdogs,
And those looking for something better.

My parents,
One reclaiming his roots
The other for love and a better life for their children.
Not giving up
Welcomed or not,
Established a home
with compassion and love.

Grateful for my upbringing,
Raised Catholic but

given the support and freedom to explore.
Because life is but so much more.

To discover myself and become
The best person I can be.
One that would make my parents proud
Just as I am of them.

For the long-forgotten stories
Rising among the ashes.
My family's struggles, their roots, their everlasting existence.

Humble, loving, and kind,
Stubborn, independent
And one of a kind.
Work ethic reflecting those famous, ringing words
Si se puede,
All is possible.

But our first lesson,
The importance of familia,
An unbreakable bond.
Stronger and better together,
My family is what I'm grateful for.

Darlene Cervantes

By Amber Shatto
Username: healer

Gratitude

There is no simple answer to what there is to be grateful for
This question does not have just one answer, it means so much more
There is so much to be grateful for in life, more than I can explain
First and foremost, I am grateful for the life experiences that cause pain
These pains show us what happiness truly is
It shows us that perspective can reveal the true meaning behind pure bliss
Life and the Universe are what I am grateful for
The Universe is the reason why I have my mother and father, whom of which is a part of my core

The love and support of my mother are what helped me to develop my sense of self
The pains and sorrows of my father are the reasons why I am so pushed to help
The ability to have free will and to be able to think for myself
The reason we have these things is from the Universe and it is responsible for life itself
I am grateful for nature and the ability to breathe
And the ideas and thoughts that I am able to conceive
I could go on and on about what there is to be grateful for
But this short list explained is just the beginning of what is to be really explored

Amber Shatto

By Bailey Gausling
Username: kittyybaileyy

Simply Grateful

I'm grateful for
sunshine seeping into my skin like a vitamin D-infused tea
flowing through my pores
for water droplets that ooze from cotton candy snow clouds
on rainy days
which reminds me of similar water droplets, salty tears I
have secreted from welled eyes that race down my face,
sometimes like a rapid river other times a light drizzle
regardless of the pour or the saddened emotion, it's an
action of the living
The dead have no more tears left to cry, and I am thankful
that I can feel
Even at times when the feelings are not the best

I am grateful for my family and friends
as they make the obstacles in my life feel like a playground
Every rerun of the same lesson turns into a carousel
Every time I couldn't walk they made me believe it was just
a game of hopscotch
Every imbalanced catastrophe was just a seesaw supported
by a single pivot point
Every change in life was just another swing on a monkey bar
and when I felt like I was falling seconds
near hitting the hardened charcoaled cement they were
there to pick
me right back up and carry my body towards the canvas of
blue that covers the sky
so that my fingertips could grip firmly onto the next bar,
encouraging me to keep swinging
because there is a new perspective on the other side
I am grateful I have recognized there is another side to see,
to experience, and to cherish

I am grateful for my furry friends
when 2 pm turned into 2 am and I still hadn't left my bed
their purrs and cuddles assured me that sometimes it's okay
to have days like this,
but not a week like this because they still need food and water
I am grateful for food and water
For the fuel in my body that keeps the engine turning on so
that I make it to my next destination

I am grateful for my body, she works 24 hours 7 days a
week, never stopping
just to make sure I am still alive so that I can simply live
I am grateful for life and everything it has to offer
from the highest of the mountains to the depths of the deep
blue sea
I am grateful to put this pen to this paper so that I can do
the other thing that keeps me alive, writing
I am grateful for poetry and for words and for language
and for finding purpose within the realm of this infinitely
crazy world
I am grateful to be me
in this present moment,
in my past moments,
and for all the moments there are to come
I am simply grateful, forever and always

Kitty Bailey

By Michelle Ruby
Username: shelle-belle

Growing With Gratitude

I'm grateful for my life even when I can't quite feel my purpose. I somehow just know that is a gift. The colors of the sky and the beauty of nature each morning when I wake up. I'm grateful for my Grandmother and her loving arms and guidance. For her health and her unconditional love. Her arms and her hugs. Her wisdom and her patience.
I'm grateful for my grown children, each day my heart swells even more with pride.
I'm grateful for the hugs, the hikes,and the laughter as well as the memories that we have all shared. I'm grateful for the man that stands by my side, who stepped up when the others stepped away. He stayed. He stayed.
I'm grateful for my pets, for the soft and gentle kisses and nudges of support when I am often too overwhelmed and

emotional to see the bright side. They pull me back and ground me. It's unconditional love at its finest.

I'm grateful for my GOD because without him, I wouldn't be here today. I'm grateful for second chances and the lessons that I have learned along the way.

I'm grateful for the birds and the wild animals as they sing their beautiful songs.

I'm grateful for the doctors that fix me when I can't go on.

I'm grateful for the strangers that become friends and the presence of angels in my time of need.

I'm grateful for family. Distant and close by. I'm grateful for my beautiful cousin. She is my hero. She saved my heart and gave me peace when I was absolutely dying inside.

I'm grateful for my kind heart, and for my strength. For being determined to survive.

I'm grateful for the dreamers. The encouragers and those that gently push.

I'm grateful for my counselor as she helps me take my control back and gives me the confidence to keep pushing on.

I'm grateful for the unsealed family who write tender and vulnerable stories from their hearts.

I'm grateful for their transparent and beautiful hearts.

Shelle

By Tatyana Roscoe
Username: taty5229

Great-Full

Time has allowed me to receive perspective like an opportunity. I learned to be selfless which helped me to be reflective.
I remember the battles, back when I was unsure about what mattered. Hard lessons battered my soul until a diamond emerged. Now as an adult I can speak on what I'm grateful for.

Full of melanin so perseverance is my friend.
The puppeteer pulling strings helping me to live. Imagine the odds I had to beat just to get here. Minimal control, I'm grateful for the soul. Naturally magnetic, I'm appreciative in regards to my aesthetics. Life is a present and the present is a gift.

Manifesting dreams is my elective to pick. Existing on this plain with grace exceeds feeling great. Fully capable of giving praise every day. Compared to the world I am a decimal ok? I have no control within the flow of the world. Grateful for my awareness, senses were awakened now she's articulating.

I'm speaking on frequencies I hope the readers can hear me. Crisp and pristine, I am grateful for poetry. Speaking for myself, when it comes to my health, I am grateful.
I have too much to say in relation to this word. Recently realizing I have a lot to be grateful for.

ThePoetess

By Clementine Pallanca
Username: clementinepallancagmail-com

Lucky

It feels like an early morning in a drizzly forest
where Nature wakes up with grace and the birds are singing
to celebrate the possibilities of the new day.
It warms my heart every time I think about the trust we
share and the unconditional love you offer.
I met you on my life's darkest road
And you helped me through it to find a better and stronger
version of myself.
I am eternally grateful for your precious presence,
My sweet dog.

CP

By Jonathan Odle
Username: jlodle11

The Power Of Choice

We can suffer a loss and fall.
We can pick ourselves up and stand tall.
We can let others make us feel small.
We can let their words have no effect on us at all.
We can choose to do nothing.
We can choose to be something.
We can live life unclean.
We can even pursue our dreams.
We can do things alone.
We can be part of a team.
We can walk beside hate.
We can run, full of love.
We can live our lives restrained.
We can fly free, like a dove.

We can drown in sadness.
We can sing and rejoice.
What am I most grateful for?
The power that lies inside of every choice.

Jonathan Odle

By Arela Williams
Username: arelawilliams

Eye Of The Storm

What kind of water is this?
It's been 8 months, but it seems like only yesterday I was hysterically begging my body for forgiveness.

I'm sorry!
I'm sorry!
I'm sorry!

Waves crashed into my cheeks, too loud to hear me accept my own apology.

Already too exposed to hide
I had no choice but to face this flood of grief and sorrow.

Unsure if I could make it to the eye of the storm, my mind had to decide.

Sink or swim?
Sink or swim?
Sink or swim?

Thankfully a whispering wind offered the current of Neutral Jing.

Float.
Ride.
Sail nothing.

At least there is no pressure to decide.
A buoyant body waiting to wash up onto the warm sands of compassion.
The day I no longer see my own vessel as a weapon formed against me.

Hopefully that day comes.

Today,
Like clockwork, the water met my eyes for the some thousandth time, but to my surprise…

Thank you!
Thank you!
Thank you!

I heard it clearly, from me to me:
I know we have no energy
to swim,
But thank you for enough resilience not to sink
And enough acceptance to transform self-hate into a sunrise.
I'm not sure what kind of water this is,
But I'm grateful we're afloat.

Azela Williams

By Soriah McClendon
Username: msriahsankofa

Peace That Passes All Understanding

For peace of God, which surpasses all understanding
For this has guarded my heart and mind
Helping me walk on my lonesome journey to my
purpose divine
To travel to a world consumed by the dark, to be a beacon
of light, always shall we fight?
For a new release of this identity that has always been forced
upon me
They thought that the power of love was a weakness
Trapped away beat and molded to be shy and meek
Then hide behind religious foes
equilibrium balanced which leads us into our accountability
we must unfold

Sadly they did not know, the pressure applied helped the collective ascend and fly
Oh how they prayed for my demise
But God wrote otherwise
For I have found my peace, for this knowledge has been applied
This essence that you feel from me has been uniquely assigned
Focused my energies
To achieve God's gifted divinity
Releasing the pain so imprisoned within me
For I have received my liberty
Blessings be to all the souls that long to be free…

Soriah Sankofa McClendon

By Taylor Rose
Username: tvigil12

The Giving Of A Blessed Life

The way the dirt folds
beneath my feet
reminding me,
Just how far I've walked
Like my grandmother before me.

The way you held my hand
And told me stories.
Unknowingly forging
the path that lay ahead of me.

Endlessly grateful
for all the days
For all the ways

that you taught me to live
my truth, my story.

Words written now
in permanent ink,
I carry forever with me.
"The giving of a blessed life."
Your greatest gift to me.

This life I cherish.
The time we've shared.
This path you've forged.

The memories you've given me.

Forever grateful,
Is all that I will ever be.
For God gave you to me.

Even for just a brief moment,
in this eternity.

Forever grateful,
Is all that I will ever be.

Taylor Rose

By Krystana Mayers
Username: kay

My Chameleon

A chameleon takes many forms in this world

An entity, that is very personal to me, has that same property

The way it can morph into many unique facets is endless

This being enables me to take in the soft air that expands my lungs

The air that's clean, all around me and allows me to see another day

Part of this creature has my face, is a bit older, wiser and is who I call 'mom'

Another part of it has an equal amount of age and wisdom, with more masculine behavior, and is who I call 'dad'

It is mixing lemon-zest ginger tea with a detox formula of cinnamon, cardamom and dandelions

Reveling in the subtle taste of each herb

And noticing that the tang of the lemon is surprisingly overshadowed by the subtle sweetness of its cardamom-dominated partner

This abstract wonder is going to my sister's house

Worrying that I might clash with her womb mate, my other sister, as I often do

And having those worries dissipate as soon as an intoxicating liquid touches my lips

And mountains of food make a home in my stomach

This hidden beast is vividly imagining anything from butterflies in my backyard to everything
I want Jason Diaz and Keith Powers to do to me

And letting my penmanship kiss endless papers as I let each and every intricate detail run wild because my passion is infinite when written

This sought-after figure is the beauty and self-sufficiency that becomes me each and every day

It is when I see good company that I haven't seen in years but become blessed with the best sense of reminiscence towards

This rarity is a family to cook, pray and share endless meals, stories and laughter with on days not limited to Thanksgiving

This joy is cherishing the fortunes I have been given

This chameleon, with all the layers it possesses, is known as gratitude

Kmayers

By Justina Madelaine

Mercury's Sincerity

I know pain because I know love.
Pain & love can be the most powerful or disastrous recipe known by man.
Between the two, I sometimes contemplate which carries heaviest within the heart.
Some place armor to protect themselves.
Others allow the knife to slowly seep underneath their skin.
"Always sleep with one eye open.
Never take anything for granted."
This can be torturous within itself —
how can we ever get any real sleep?
Are my eyes not for me?
Are your eyes for you?
For what we see, are we really seeing for what it is?

Pain deludes within the soul.
Love delights within the truth.
May our eyes rest peacefully through the most somber of nights.
Where darkness resides there is light to be found.
I choose to sleep with my eyes closed.
There is beatitude in trusting the madness.
For I choose to love on and appreciate for what I do have, rather than what I do not.
May this spirit I have, be the lighthouse for those that cannot make direction.
For I know being aimless very well.
May those who find me, hold me as I will do for them.
May our hearts be stoned no more.
May the love be enough even for when it may seem very little.
I know pain & I know love,
for in those I choose to be grateful for it all.

Justina Madelaine

By Brianna Rund Gange
Username: mythicalme

Thank You For Keeping My Existence My Beautiful Boy — A Poem Dedicated To My Cat

Your crystal clear caramel eyes
Meet my dull drained dark eyes

You pur to me as I feel your fur

You see the light in me before I might

Your eager for attention affection admiration

Keeps me alive.

But little do you know it's something deeper to me.

When I sing you a lullaby of words you'll never understand.
You're better than any other man.

As I feed you a can of salmon

My dark dull drained eyes start to glisten

Feeling giddy

For I am ever so grateful and thankful.

You keep me alive.

Brianna Rund

By Ashelyn Knight
Username: ashelynknight

You

The moon and stars
The comets that sweep the sky
The sun that rises in the morning

The deer that play in the fog
The birds singing in the morning sun
The bugs doing their best day by day

My dog who greets me every day
My cat who meows at every given chance
My family that supports us

The love and support you give me
The quiet days and the playful days with you

The smile you give me when things are okay

But most of all, you.
You make me grateful.
You.

Ashelyn Knight

By Tasha Uliano
Username: tashafierce

Being Seen

When I realized he could see me,
the way I use humor as a distraction.
The way I crave love,
even though I hide from the world.
When he lovingly pointed out the parts of me
that I thought I've been hiding so well,
I melted.
I feel naked,
I feel seen.
Being seen is better than being loved.
Many men will have loved me by this time,
the version of me they've created in their head.
For that reason, it's always been a dead end.
Few people have really seen me.

Most see what they want to see,
what they want me to be
what they thought I could be,
if I was just a little less stubborn.

This is different.
This is real and raw.
That's what I saw.

I see him, too.

Tasha

By Camille Morris
Username: cmorris96

Silence.

Dear anxious thoughts,

I finally found it
halfway through a cup of Earl Grey
against the porcelain of a just used dish
in the far echoes of birds' quaint chirping
while strolling through the park
Quiet
The hush of a mind settling into serenity.

Some people don't think
rather
their minds are not incessant
forced to endure a constant monologue
seeking at every moment to be heard
Thought is intentional
a conscious effort.

My mind has always had a habit of running ahead of me
chasing fragments of ideas
pieces of abstraction that will never be whole
Body follows quick
heart racing
breath quickening
muscles tight
painful tension
Forced into incessant suffering
mentally, physically, emotionally
normal meant nothing more
than the desperate need to be free.

Then exhaustion
overwhelm finally winning me over
my body made stillness where it refused to be found
a clear rejection to so much stimuli
and laying in the quiet
created by a body truly weary
I found relief.

Now knowing this peace
I build mindfulness into my everyday
times of quiet
of tranquility
of the beauty in internal
silence.

Camille

By Alexis Bixler
Username: kiddbixx

Grateful Memories

I am grateful for the memories of you that weren't lobotomized.
For all the wounds I walked away with-
For the scars that took their places.

I am grateful for the garden that you grew in me-
After being buried in the yard.
Resilient are the flowers that grow from unforgiving earth

I am grateful for the love I give so openly.
The same love I gave to you.
The kind of love you could never reciprocate.
I felt your unprecedented apathy and hate.

I am grateful that you showed me what love isn't.
With that lesson I found my confidence.
The same confidence you replaced with insecurities.
I see now that time with you was just a ripple.

I am grateful to be Scarlet Begonias —
As I'll catch someone else's eye.
But, what I am most grateful for-
Is to not be a part of the dead.

Alexis

By Victoria Dell'Elmo
Username: vdpoetry

I Am Grateful

In my twenty years of living, I have acquired a list of little things for which I am grateful. Family & friends. That's a given, though maybe not for all people. But this is about me & not you right now. I digress, family & friends — they know who they are & how much I love them. But apart from the safe answer, I am grateful for quite a few things that include the following: rainbows after rain. Gel pens that erase. Hot caramel lattes with extra espresso no matter the temperature outside. The rush of fear mixed with adrenaline whenever I stand near the edge of something. I am grateful for all of my hyper fixations of haunted animatronic lore & morally grey fictional characters whom I continually find comfort. I am grateful for home-cooked meals by my Dad over the holidays. Especially his homemade pasta, gravy, & meatballs. Yes, it's red sauce. Yes, it's a family thing. No, it's not weird. I am grateful for the way my skin marks at the slightest touch, as if I am collecting bruises like charms on a charm bracelet. They are monuments to all my moments. Speaking of bruises, I am grateful for the first boy who bruised my heart. Well, no, actually, he broke my heart. To be specific, he broke my heart exactly two weeks before my fifteenth birthday. To the boy whose heart I broke when I got tired of trying to revive something that died a while ago, your parting words, "Thank you for the memories" will forever haunt me. A permanent skeleton in my crowded closet. I am grateful for the one who saved me in a way. Your late-night conversations & quiet compliments kept me sane as I was trying to find myself again. You are the person I would have waited an eternity for to come around. However, Lady Luck was on my side for once when I indulged in my desires that night. God, I am so grateful for that good weather, that clear October sky when we stargazed out of your sedan. Gazing at constellations, I told you how I felt. Who knew that the window to heaven was through your sunroof? So of course, I am grateful that you liked me too. & I am grateful for every moment, good or bad that I have ever had because that is what brings me to you.

Victoria Dell'Elmo

By Sofia Armstrong
Username: sofiagracearmstrong

An Ode To You, My Love

To say the gratitude
I have for you
Is infinite...
Would still be an understatement

So let me attempt to paint you a better picture with the colors of my words
The bright yellow I feel for you brings such joy and ease...
The feeling of sunshine and smiles and birds in the trees
And all good things
That warm the heart in the Light

The soft pink envelopes me
Like a sweet hug and soft kiss

You comfort and hold me
I'll forever cherish this

The blue I have felt
Runs deep, as the ocean
And though I feel sad
You still come through
You lead with compassion
Through waters unknown
Bringing peace to my heart
Cool and blue

The green that's inspired in me by your vibrant ways
Feels fresh and expansive abundant and true
"Grow" you tell me
Down my roots go
Reaching
Connecting
Making things grow

The crimson I feel for you lies deep in my heart
A longing, or yearning
Felt straight from the start
Hot, excited but slightly unsure
How could this beautiful rosy dream be mine?
The feeling inside feels ancient yet known
My soul calling yours, longing to return home
Safely nested close to yours

All of these colors…
Beautiful confusion
You help me sort through them with no expectation
Of a favor returned

So yes "grateful" might be an understatement
For the one who came into my life to help change it into
something of beauty, expansion and service
Grace is your way and everyone sees it
An exemplary example of a Man Divine

A life of devotion you model so well
I long to one day be able to say I made you proud
Forever in gratitude to You, My Love.

A. Grace

By Antoinette Gonzalez
Username: algonzalez

Grateful For Motherhood

Dear Motherhood,

You were a journey I yearned to embark on for many of my childhood years. A journey I knew I had to have however, knew nothing about. Today, I have been a mother for 15 years, nearly half my life. Your are everything I dreamed of and nothing I could have ever imagined. I cry uncontrollably. I have to re-parent myself. I've seen so many different versions of me within you.
I'm most grateful for you out of all of my life experiences. I've had some of my highest highs and my lowest lows within you. You have pushed me to grow and heal. The healing journey I have experienced was because of you. You taught me that I do not have to be what the world said I would be. You've

given me so many gifts. I've watched myself and my children grow into beautiful human beings.

I've learned kindness from you. I've learned how to love me. I've learned to treasure the moments while being excited for the future. You've taught the control freak within me that she can not control anything but herself. I can not express the magnitude of gratefulness I carry within me for you. Every minute that passes I look forward to the next.

I am excited to see what the future of motherhood holds and I'm ready for everything it has to throw at me: the good, the bad, the ugly and the pretty. So I say to you, Motherhood, thank you for everything you have and continue to gift me and all the wisdom you will impart on to me.

Forever a Mother of Motherhood,

Antoinette Gonzalez

By Roxanne De Guzman
Username: roxannedg13

Strangers In Passing

I'm fifteen and my sister and I are laughing just a little too hard in the Sephora checkout line
Everything special, but nothing new; she's my best friend, and we laugh like this all the time
The older woman behind us taps me on the shoulder, kind face and a reassuring smile
Have you guys had a few too many mimosas over brunch? Because that sure is what it seems like

Now I never knew her name, and it's been too long to remember her face
But I recall her starting a conversation, and I still think about her to this day

Unseal Your Gratitude

She said we reminded her of her daughter, a government-advisor-turned-culinary-business-owner-Hallmark-cliche
And she told us to follow our dreams no matter what, even, and especially, if they change

So here I am all these years later, three weeks before quitting my first job after graduation
Trying to decide if I should find another gig or continue my education
I'm not happy; I'm lost and confused and consumed by burning, aching, throbbing indecision
Cursing who I am and who I used to be and the people who put me in this position

I'm in this stage of life right now where I can't stop making a fool of myself
Some bad things are easy to handle, but even those, I don't handle well
And I'm desperate to grow up, to be better, to right all my wrongs and come out of my shell
But I lock myself in my room, dissociative, spiraling, pushing boulders up infinite hills

I feel so stuck, I grew up with so many dreams and so much potential, oh how I wish I was more
How I wish I hadn't stopped seeing the beauty of my own life the minute misfortune showed up at my door
It's hard to be afraid, to be alone, to do everything you could have done and still come up short

I wish I picked myself back up in the moment; now I'm
sifting through sharp glass, trying to see what I can restore

I need to be unafraid to change, to leave, to believe that the
universe is ultimately kind and good
That if I do my best until there's nothing left, then this time,
it will work out like I had always hoped it would
And I need to focus more on the things that I can do, and
do them, instead of worrying about likelihood
And one day, maybe soon, I will make sense of the lessons
that I never truly understood

I'm safe here in my bubble, surrounded by love and light
and poetry to grace every empty page
And while I've started to see the beauty in this current life, I
don't think I'll be happy if I continue to play it all safe
I think the novelty is worth the trouble; the wisdom comes
when you grow with your age
And everything new is absolutely terrifying, but not nearly
as awful as the monotony of staying the same

I'm thankful for love and the changes, the sweetness of the
strangers, and the thrill of something new
The inspiration and the solid foundations, the warmth of a
home to always come back to
The motivation of the stagnation, the things we gain
in translation — the dreams, this time I know I'll see
them through

How unprompted kindness heals the weathered heart,
turning hurricanes to morning dew

The fear of uncertainty, the passing on of courage, the
comfort of strangers being kind when they didn't have to be
Everything special, and everything new; no obligation, just
a sense of community
Softening the soul, bringing down the walls, making a lover
of someone who used to think so cynically
And the strangers I've met in passing will never know just
how much the things they've said and done still mean to me

Roxanne De Guzman

By Juan Carrillo
Username: night-lad

Finding Hope After Darkness

Sitting in the manic darkness of my mind, lost in the turmoil of what I had expected life to be.
I am not a burden; I am not a waste. I have a right to live, and I have a right to love. Damn you for betraying my heart; damn you for throwing me away like trash. I deserve better. Because I am not trash!

I was sick; God damn you, I was ill, and you and your ability to justify your bad behavior is out of this universe. I did not swim in the shadows after all.

I did not give in to the darkness and was given a light to show me my story was not done. I was shown I have a purpose and a reason to go on.

I was shown that even though my mind was hurt, I was shown how to bring some calmness to the storm within my mind through the magical potion that I was bestowed.

Rebuilding from the sadness and the turmoil is a scary feat; learning that the one person you chose to bond with felt that you were disposable is not an easy act to survive, but you can stay.

I found new purpose and self-awareness with my potion of calmness, and with all of this, I found pure love in a way I never thought I would see.

I found an actual goal for my life and a closer connection with God. I found a reason to keep fighting, an excuse to keep showing up in my own life and not giving up for as long as the universe with God allows me to be. Now that I get to live in potential, I get to live in hope. And after being in the depths of darkness, this is a much better place to be.

Juan Carrillo

By Kiera Baity
Username: kierakb

Holiday Highs

surrounded by love, I feel
like a sun(ken) flower with romantics
talking in my sleep,
my day diving into a deep
both
suffocating and serene.
I'm grateful for my lungs reminding me
to finish strong…
butterflies in my body,
grunge in my bones.

Kiera Baity

171

By Dee Hainsworth
Username: deehainsworth

Friends In Transience

friends in transience
we consider what matters,
and come to the conclusion that nothing does
we rush to see the sights,
so busy being in this place that we forget to be
we grip bellies in laughter around small
tables tucked in tiny corners
we swim in the ocean,
gaining relief from our minds
we cherish our mistakes,
exchanging them like currency
we cry on balconies and in odd bunk beds,
holding one another tight
we beg for softness from one another

with our eyes,
let me hold you
let me hold you
let me hold you
we narrate entire new worlds together in bus seats at the back,
and then this and then this and then this
we toss cigarettes into one another's mouths,
giggles increased with each failed attempt
we enact characters on the metro,
delighting in one another's creativity
we consider what matters,
and come to the conclusion that everything does

Dee

By Lorie Simonian
Username: loriesim

Clarity

Oh, the world goes
thimble-sized
when I am feeling blue,

when I'm taught,
and trapped,
and tiny,

when I thrash,
and sigh,
and stew.

But in those times,
some sleeping eye

blinks open all anew;

a lovely lens
with blazing rays
which beam me up

and out the maze,
so holy wonder steeps me
in a misty, magic haze,

and absolutely
everything deserves
the highest praise:

pears and plums and
petit fours,
glasses and neckties,

bikes and boats and
bubbles floating up
in sunshine skies,

planters plows and
seedlings sprouting
through the darling dirt,

so happy for it all
that I could scarcely

dream of hurt.

Three cheers for this
tender cloud which
puffs around my heart!

Im grateful for the
piece of me that
always sees the art.

Lorie Simonian

By Jamell Crouthers
Username: aquarianmelo

Grateful For Four Things

I always tell people the most important things to life,

Being good mentally, physically, emotionally and spiritually.

It's what I'm grateful for in my life,

The journey to get to where I am currently.

Mentally where I wake up every day and feel good,

Where my mind isn't cluttered and full of uncertainty.

There's a joy and happiness to where my mind is,

Where I'm able to feel and be myself more.

Physically, I'm thankful to be healthy,

Where I can workout daily and keep my body in shape.

My body is well-rested most days and I'm energized,

I'm rejuvenated and I always feel good.

Spiritually I'm around people who bring me happiness,

Meeting people who have good energy to them.

Meeting someone who I've grown close to,

Having a spiritual connection that brings me happiness and peace.

To have my mom who brings my spirits up daily,

Sharing laughter, jokes and sometimes deep conversations about life.

To feel good emotionally where the sun shines bright,

Through the windows that fulfill my soul with views of the city I live in.

To be grateful for life's simplicities,

A home, food, clothes and people who are important to me in my life.

I'm thankful where I am in my life,

And looking forward to all that's to come in my life.

Jamell Crouthers

By Danette Byatt
Username: dbyatt

Hand Over Heart

I thank my lucky stars
For the freedom to dream.
My mind is my own.
Even when my head's
In the clouds —
Hand over heart,
I hold my dreams dearly.

One dream I dream
Is to meet my brother,
On the fluffiest of clouds.
His mind is now his own.
He has dreamt of me too —
Hand over heart,
That I hold him dearly.

As long as I dream
I create,
And be with those I love.
They are not just stories
But a part of me —
Deep in my heart,
That I hold so dearly.

So dream I will,
And dream I must.
Embrace this freedom
If not to love others,
Then to love myself —
As it is my own heart,
That I hold so dearly.

Danette

By Lorinda Boyer
Username: lorinda

Thank You, Stonewall

Parade participants dance and gyrate.
Snaking down the glittery rainbow street.
While drag queens sashay perfectly straight
Atop outrageously high heels, an incredible feat.

My eyes dart wildly from side to side.
Taking in ample amounts of bare skin
Of people unconcerned with a need to hide.
Of strangers marching closer than kin.

I breathe in the thickly weed-scented air.
Feel the heat from the scorching asphalt.
I toss back my head without a care.
Unafraid of danger or assault.

On this particular day
There's no hate for loving my own gender.
Surrounded by all the gay,
Love reigns in abundant splendor.

Five million gather to say thank you
For fifty years of Stonewall's disquiet.
To honor and attest that which we hold true.
And to remember the first pride was a riot.

Lorinda Boyer

By Harley Schechter
Username: harleyschechter

Losing And Choosing A Sister

The grass isn't greener
On this side of the fence
It's dry and crunchy
When you take a step
Life over here is
Nowhere close, to perfect

But we've got lawn chairs
And the blender works great
Tiny umbrellas in our drinks
We have good music and
Morbid jokes
We have each other
When you don't

One day the clouds
Will roll in
To water our grass
The drought will pass
Turning our yard back to green

But for now, we'll stay here
In the scorching heat
Keeping each other company.

Harley Schechter

By Ashleigh Ogg
Username: ashes478

Grateful

I asked my mother what she was grateful for
She said "well honey that would be you"
So I asked my father what he was grateful for
And he said "you, and your mother too"
So then I turned to my lover, and asked him the
same question
He said "my family, my friends, my cat and video games"
Then I gathered my friends, and started a procession

I asked what were they were grateful for?
Please bare your heart to mine
And they answered, from their core
As they walked on down the line
They said "I'm grateful for my family

With all the mess they can be"
They said "I'm grateful for my homies
Who are always there for me"
They said "I'm grateful for my pets"
And a bunch of other stuff
They said "Ash, you're the best,
Come on and walk with us"

They said "enough about me, let's talk about you"
Oh, but there's nothing to say, you've already said it all
"Stop avoiding the question, it's kind of rude
And surely, we haven't covered it all"
So I took a deep breath, and looked at all my friends
And raised my voice so that all could hear
I'll walk with you, until the very end
Because it's you that I hold most dear

When I found my parents, hidden in the crowd
I said I've always been grateful for you,
And I hope I've made you proud
And tell everyone else in our family, too
There's still someone else I haven't found

When I got to my lover, his family was there
So I told them I was grateful for all that they've done
My love wouldn't be here without their care
And Christmas has never been so much fun
I looked to my lover, said don't feel left out

I'm so grateful for you, with all my heart
I simply don't think I could go without
Another one of your delectable tarts

As the sun began to set, descending into the night
I gathered my family and friends all around
And their pets, video games, all their delights
Just for a minute, the time is now
I must tell you what I am most grateful for
Since I asked you, it is only fair I offer up
My own reply, to those I adore:

I am grateful for my mother, because my father is too
I am grateful for your families, because you are too
I am grateful for all the animals we keep,
Simply because they are in our coop
I am grateful for my lover,
Because he loves me too
I am grateful for the planets,
The stars and the moons
Crap, now it's a tangent
I'll wrap it up soon

Let's enjoy ourselves now, let's have a good time
You, me, and all the stuff we like
If we could have one giant party, that would be alright
All that I am grateful for is here tonight

Ashleigh Ogg

By Olivia Droddy
Username: od

What I Am Most Grateful For

As we near the end of this challenging year,
I reflect on the smiles, the laughs, and the tears.

There is so much to be grateful for, but one thing stands out in my mind,
It's my Mother — woman so strong and sweet and beautiful and kind!

You see, almost 23 years ago, my Mom adopted me, a baby girl.
And she is my true hero, my comforter, and my whole entire world!

I appreciate her patience when I'm not doing well.

She's reached out a hand when I've stumbled and picked me up when I fell!

I am so grateful for her, she's so special, I'd even give my life,
I remain grateful despite the hardships and the strife!

Yes, I am most grateful for my Mother!
I love that warm feeling I get when we embrace each other!

And although one day, she and I may be physically apart,
I'll always be most grateful for her and her special place in my heart!

Olivia M. Droddy

By Jazmine Greene
Username: ladygreene47

———————

Heterosexual Life Partner

When I think of the things in my life that
I am grateful for there is so much
But one of the things that comes to mind
Is a person

When I think of what a best friend should be she is what
comes to mind

People hurt you
They disappoint you
Make you disbelieve

When the truth is right in front of you
You have to see it for what it truly is

And that is gratefulness because to understand the importance of
a good person, good friend

Can be once in a lifetime

To find a soul mate in a friend
Is special

To create a bond of trust
To share honestly
Even when I don't like it
But I always ended up needing it

A pair of misfits
A lifetime of laughter

Silliness
Sadness
The good and bad and everything inbetween

Joyful
Thoughtful
Weirdly unique

No matter what always there

I love person and I will forever be thankful
To call my friend

Jazmine Greene

By Jessica Conner
Username: milkyjessi

Eileen

Fingers loosened hold on fragile glass that shattered into fragmented pieces in front of me
But these fingers also held yours as you took your last breaths in the physical world

Teeth Bones arranged in a clustered pattern with asymmetry
The same teeth that get exposed when I replay our memories
Teeth that work overtime when chewing taffy
The sweet tooth you also possessed

Hair I can never manage to keep in the state I left the house in
Was the first thing you lost when the treatment began

Strangers in grocery lines spilling their hearts over canned soup

You would tell me all the people that stopped you along the way too
Gravitational pull that made one fall into your orbit
Collector of people's secrets
My warmth is a borrowed gift
I will never see parts myself without finding you

Jessica Conner

By Chloe Mayer
Username: lostinthesound7

Once Lost, Now Found

I am grateful
That through pain that seemed unbearable
Wrapped tightly in the sabotage of comforting vices
Obscured by wreckage of my past selves
Deep in the alcoves of my mind, last lit long ago —
I found my voice

Vagabond with a Voice

By Kiore
Username: kiorea

Gratitude For Humanity

Let me start by saying this

I'm grateful for the sun and the wind, even when it feels brisk

I'm grateful I'm able to inhale air that won't make me feel sick

I'm grateful I'm able to open my eyes each day, move my arms and legs, and have functioning ears to listen to as many songs as I'd like on replay

I'm grateful for those in my life because without them, I'd be putting up a strong fight

I'm grateful to be able to have an opportunity like this

It's shocking how many of these in the past I've missed

I'm grateful that I'm still able to stand strong after all that I have been through

Grateful for my strong resilience, that played a big part in getting me through

I'm grateful to see every day as a new opportunity

I'm grateful to know that everything I am desiring is within me

Regardless of what I'm told to do by society

Standing strong in my truth will only free me

I give my gratitude for the privilege that I have

Unfortunately, to so many others, privilege is something they lack

They're too busy fighting a war they don't want, trying to come up for air after impact

So I give gratitude every day because that could have easily been me

Still struggling to understand why such horrible things are happening

Imagine being a child unable to live a normal life

All because of those higher than you do not want to take into consideration your life

The life that you just started, the life that you so rightfully deserve to live

But can't because they want to make sure you don't continue to exist

So I'm grateful to have a voice to speak for those who don't

And block out the judgment of those who won't

I'm grateful to be a part of a world that can make a difference if we want

By being aware & raising our voices, we can become the antidote

I'm grateful to admit that yes, I do feel guilty

Because change happens when you start to take accountability

When you allow yourself to embody humility

Your ego and pride have no choice but to dissipate

So I'm grateful to be one of the few who will be a part of the long overdue change

Even if that means it won't happen until I'm 98

I'm grateful for the opportunities and blessings that have yet to come my way

But are already headed to me so all I need to do is wait patiently

And continue to face the challenges that will arrive

So that they're able to find their way much more easily

I'm grateful to know that I choose to do something differently than those around me

I'm grateful to believe that my voice is important, so hear me clearly as I say this loudly

You get what you give out, so do so wisely

Never hold yourself back, be authentically yourself proudly

Always remember patience is a rare commodity

So slow down, and relax — there is no need to rush it, honestly

Your time will come when you are taken seriously

But be sure to accept that you'll be the light most won't want to see

By embracing all that you are & all that you will be

Your world will turn upside down in the best way possible

Giving you this message will go down as one of my good deeds

Because sharing prior knowledge with others is one hundred percent free

And giving gratitude rewards my life more abundantly

Which in return skyrockets the security & confidence in me

To continue to stand up for those who cannot stand on their own two feet

Kiove Andrews

By Gerald Washington
Username: lostone89

Being Able To Be Grateful

Dear Unsealers,

Being grateful is something that I don't do enough
especially when life is rough
but when the grateful spirit enters the mind
A great wave of gratitude gives me joy inside

There are so many things I'm grateful for
and have me eager to see what more
life has in store

I'm grateful every day to have another chance
and to start a new dance
I'm grateful for another day to choose
even when I have the blues

I'm grateful that I was given the blessing of life
even though it's filled with constant strife
I'm grateful for the life experiences that I've had
Some happy and some deeply sad

I'm grateful that I'm in a different place
when years ago, my head was in a different space
I'm grateful for the many connections I've made
some connections remained, while others faded away

I'm grateful for the achievements I've accomplished so far
they make me feel that it's possible to reach the stars
And I'm grateful to be in a position to be able
to express feeling grateful

Gerald Washington

By Maggie Faye
Username: maggiefaye

I Am Grateful For Blue Skies

I'm grateful for blue skies, warm sunshine, and a breeze that kisses the nose.
I'm grateful for green grasses and rushing creeks and bare feet.
I'm grateful for friends and lovers that grab you by the hand and dance with you.
I'm grateful for their consistent reminders, "You're safe here. I love you."
I'm grateful for the forehead kisses my love gives me,
And that he bends down to let me kiss his forehead right back.
I'm grateful for the safety of my home, and I'm grateful for a newcomer's compliments,
"It looks like a gallery in here!" Thank you, the art is my favorite, too.

I'm grateful, especially for the rabbit posed in play, a floppy handstand,
That's been in our home longer than my memories. It's one of my first ones.
I'm grateful for the way the sun shines into my mother's bedroom just before sunset in spring.
It bathes the house in gold and it's one of the most beautiful things I've ever seen.
I'm grateful for the drums that echo in my chest at the concert in Alpharetta,
And the music that reverberates in my bones. I'm grateful to have a body that feels the music.
It's exhilarating and soothing, an ecstasy I don't need to swallow.
I'm grateful for cats with soft fur and who love love love ear scratches.
I'm grateful to my body and my brain for giving me the gift of sensation.
Even when it's too much, or not enough, I'm grateful to be present to feel.

Maggie Faye

By Devananda Vargas
Username: devananda

Letter To A Friend

If every person we encounter and meet is simply a reflection of ourselves and we will be attracted to the qualities and attributes of that person that we desire/aspire to in our lives or that we already possess and like, and we will judge or dismiss those that we find ourselves repulsed by, then meeting strangers and making friends is just another way to practice yoga in this thing we call life.

So, friend, as I fall more in love with myself every day I fall more in love with you.

You are unlike any friend I've met on my journey to date.

I am deeply attracted to my reflection in you as this is the first time in my life I've been so in love with my body, my mind, my soul — you are the closest reflection to my authentic self I've yet found. Yes, in all the glorious imperfections of what got us here.

I am forever grateful to the universe for creating this time, this place, this space for me to meet you/me. It has been exactly what I didn't know I needed. You have made my mind and soul bloom in adoration, anticipation and expectation for where I have been, and where I am headed next.

Thank you for being you, and for holding space for me. Thank you for being vulnerable, for sharing your story, for creating a safe and encouraging place free from judgment for me to explore my thoughts, feelings and beliefs — to be authentically me.

May we celebrate what we learned about each other and ourselves during these five weeks.

May we find comfort in our hearts going forward knowing that this version of ourselves shared a sacred space together and let this version of ourselves live here in this memory in infamy.

May we joyfully move on to the next time, place and space to explore with curiosity and if it should be, meet up again to check in, compare notes and celebrate once more.

May we be happy. May we be healthy. May we live with ease.

Cheers

Devananda Vargas

By Aimee Concepcion
Username: aimeevc

11:11

I used to make a wish on 11:11. But now the time goes by and I don't even bat an eye, because I used to wish for you and I. You are the shooting star I wished on when I was young , the birthday candles I blew out on my 23rd birthday, the penny I threw in the fountain, you are everything I asked for and more. How did I get so lucky? Was it all the wishing and fishing in the sea of all the people I've ever met, I'd make a bet they'd think it's luck. But the reality is I had to fight for you. Fight the demons at night that held me so tight. They told me I wasn't worthy of love and that everyone else would be put above, that is until you showed up. Your green eyes and perfect smile just in time to drive me wild but somehow also make me feel calm and protected. All the times I went fishing in the sea of people when in reality you were the whole ocean and all I had to do was look up , and I guess that's why they called it luck. I don't know what to wish for on 11:11 because you already feel like heaven.

Aimeevc

By Jameela Dompier
Username: jameela

A Gentle Reminder From Friends

when i feel myself losing my gratitude, i turn to my dearest friends

i step into the sun that shines, despite everything it must bear witness to

its warmth welcomes the waking grass who grows, despite those who would carelessly trudge across

the grass, home to creatures big and small, existing just as they are meant to, despite the growing and changing world around them

and as the sun shines and the grass grows, the wind flows
carrying the birds who sing songs of sorrow solemnly,
despite the noisy chaos of humanity

this harmony, so gracious and unrelenting, exist perfectly
so, asking nothing of me and giving me everything in return

i am grateful for the companionship, the steadiness,
the reminder

i am grateful, i am grateful, i am grateful
thank you, thank you, thank you

Jameela Dompier

By Mary Freeman
Username: dayoldpastries

Holding On

I always knew you were good

I tried and I tried to hold on
Till my fingers bled
And my soul all but drowned
I thought I would fall
I thought I would lose you
But something held me there
Something made me stick
There was a piece of thread that was stronger
Than the rest of the rope that had been ripped to shreds
It was you
You held on because I asked you to
Even when I was pissed at you and yelled at you

And pushed you to the edges of my mind
You held on because I asked you to
Even when I thought you didn't love me and I
Forgot the ways you've shown me how well you know me
You held on because I asked you to
You've always had the strength that I lack
You've always had the patience I couldn't wait for
You've always seen what I pretended to be blind to
I almost let the world convince me that you're not good
But I could never fully believe them like I do you
I just needed someone to speak my language
To help me understand
To prove what I always knew in the depths of
My heart, mind and soul
Thank you for holding on

I always knew you were good

Mary Renee Freeman

By Nicholas Grogan
Username: nrgrogan

Riviera Paradise: A Poem Inspired By My Stepfather On His Last Birthday

A somewhat troubled family,
disjointed and unusual-
sit in a lake house celebrating two birthdays,
my stepfather's and mine.

Both days close together,
but emotions always miles apart.

This celebration is different-
unfamiliar notes and frequencies
fill the air-
Gut wrenching laughter!

Mom's got a promotion,
Stepdad uncharacteristically soft and proud.

his combat armor off and weapon laid on the ground.
His battle against us is finally over.

He looks at me
and I see him for the first time,
the man he always could have been,
and I let my guard down.

He asks if I could write a poem about this weekend.
I know exactly what to say:

It's those quiet moments,
when an outer body experience
drowns out the raucous
times we typically spend together.
those moments when full glasses of
champagne —complemented
by the pitter patter of
jovial children
and tipsy adults-
fill your home.

And you take a moment,
to look at it all,
a still image
saved in your mind like a photograph,
capturing the essence of why
you are you,

and how fortunate you are
to have who you have in your life.

And you are thankful.
For at least in this moment in time,
you were able to capture and place this photo
at the front of your picture book.

Nicholas Grogan

By Mira Catlin
Username: miraculous88

Blessed With Gratitude

The blessings given to me by the word gratitude:
Giving spirit
Relationships with others
Able-bodied
Trusting others when in doubt
Imagination
Tough situations with lessons to learn
Understanding others without judgment
Desire to be a blessing towards others,
Enjoying the life I have been given, even when some days are harder than others.

Mira Catlin

By Emily Elder
Username: poewrote

The Ups And Downs Of Family

What am I thankful for?
I'm thankful for those who stuck around,
When I secretly lost my battle
And I got my second chance,
And they were still there...

Thankful for the ones who stood firm,
When my love lost their battle,
Without the second chance
And I'm thankful for the ones
Who knew to just be there,
When words couldn't bring comfort.

I'm thankful for the pushes,
When sounds couldn't move mountains

Thankful for the hugs,
That brought me out.

Thankful for the look in their eyes,
That said one day it'll be alright.
And maybe you'll never be fine,
But you'll learn to fight...
And that'll get you through the night.

Thankful for the mother who never gave up,
The text from him that begged for an answer
To bring me back
And thankful for the shoulders lent to cry on,
When tissues couldn't hold my tears.

Emily A. Elder

By Rebecca Engle
Username: rengle3

The Journey

In the ever-changing dance of life, I find myself surrounded by reasons to be grateful. Each day, I am presented with a vibrant tapestry of experiences that remind me to appreciate the little things.

College is like an exhilarating adventure, where knowledge thrives and dreams are nurtured. It's a place where friendships bloom like stars, illuminating the nights with laughter and love. These cherished moments with friends bring me endless joy.

My family is my sanctuary, providing unwavering support and serving as the glue that holds everything together. And then there's my boyfriend, a guiding light through life's waves. His warmth and love create an anchor where my heart finds solace.

Life throws hurdles our way, testing our strength and resilience. But it's within these challenges that we truly discover our inner power. Embracing these hurdles becomes a testament to our resilience and marks the beginning of new journeys.

I am grateful for the gentle kiss of each sunrise, for a love that grows deeper with every passing day, for those moments of pure bliss. In this symphony called life, gratitude soars like the notes played on a beautiful melody. I hold onto all that I cherish, now and for all time.

Rebecca Engle

By Tamara Gallagher
Username: tgal

Many Stories That Made Me

You hear so many stories that end with
"that could of been me"
"That could of been my reality"

You hear so many stories
That end opposite
Of what happened to you

I was born 1 pound 9 ounces at 26 weeks
With my twin sister who didn't make it unfortunately
Yet I am sitting here as a 30-year-old woman
With a family of my own

You hear so many stories

of a predator being around a kid
taking advantage of them in their youth
when they feel they are being cornered
they do something to cover their tracks
leaving that child without breath

yet I'm sitting in front of you
a product of child abuse
not only physically
sexually at a young age
yet, I'm still here to say
I survived, I am willing to speak for them
those who didn't make it out of the abuse the predator
inflicted

you hear so many stories
as the young girl gets older
she digs deeper to fill an emptiness inside
that she tries to fill that void with a guy
since she never knew the right way to love
she thought that abuse was a sign he cared

I sit here and think
despite the abuse I received
despite my mental woes
I was able to marry a man who cares
who treats me like a queen
gives me everything I need

was willing to be patient
from 19 years old he held me in his arms
wouldn't let go
now 30, with 3 beautiful kids
laughter ringing in our ears
from the moment we awake
until we go to sleep
rising back up the next day
to do it all again

you hear so many stories
of a couple living with their parents
struggling to make it out of there family's house

yet after a few years
we were able to pay off our debt
being accepted, like I was their own daughter
they gave me a place to lay my head
we rode the bus and walked carrying groceries
they never judged in any way
they planned our wedding
shared so much love
until one day we are able to say
we moved out our parents' home
into our own space

I am able to pull up to our apartment
we have called home for 3 years

accumulated 4 reliable vehicles in those years
a house we can call our own
stability at jobs we've had for years
accumulating so many skills
moving from hourly to salary
able to give our kids everything they need
so they can thrive inside our home
sharing their light everywhere they go

you hear so many stories
many being called by the Lord
yet they do not answer the door

despite what felt like a crumbling foundation
my husband going to the military
I heard the call The Lord spoke to me
I answered and He began working with me
although my husband was miles away
he was also being worked on by The Lord
I began writing again
finding a gift I left a long time ago
I began writing for The Lord
I prayed to Him and asked
what am I supposed to do with this gift of my hands?

He spoke through my mom who called
right after I said amen

told me that I was suppose to write poetry Autobiography
about my life
we hung up and tears poured down my face
I asked him to help me tell my story
it won't be easy, but I'm willing to do it
if He gives me the words to write
I read my Bible and fasted
for months poems came to me on my drive to work
I wrote them down once I parked
writing poetry Autobiography that's personal to me
has always been my lifelong dream

by then my husband came home
he helped me find a way to publish through Amazon
break free was the title that rang in my ears
I was able to heal from so much baggage at hand
now my family is together again
we began to melt as one
finding peace in each other's arms
with support in our family's bubble
growing day by day as we shared our stories
on our individual journeys

baseball games and championship wins
going to a airshow my husband showed the Chinook
proud family smiles we all shared
as I look back and think
I have so much growth to be thankful for

so much life I've got to live
finding my purpose along the way
discovering my voice inside the rain

it's not one thing I'm grateful for
it's not one person I want to give thanks to
I feel grateful to be standing here
despite what the day brings
I am living life abundantly
with love that flows in every vein
lineage and wealth from the depth of our souls

laughter and personalities that light up rooms
testimonies that will cause tears to stream
divine protection in every season
tests and lessons that break the mold
creating a new path for the next generations to go

I am so grateful for many things
a list that can go on for days
before my head hits my bed
I pray a prayer of gratitude
it all started as a thought on your head
that you know every hair that lies upon my head
the path that I was always meant to go
the bumps upon the road
you knew it all and went ahead

I am eternally grateful for your divine timing and presence you bring
I will walk down the straight and narrow path
following your light that shines so bright

I thank you for the love I give
the lessons I learn from my kids
the love and protection my husband gives
the bright smiles I receive
the affirming words they bring
I am in awe when it comes to my life at hand
I wake up happy despite what plays in my head
there is no other place I'd rather be
than here at home with my family
praising you in every moment
building a relationship while you're molding
me into the vessel you always called me to be
I am at peace you have brought my being

Mara Gallagher

By Hannah Gonneville
Username: hangon

A Song Of Thanksgiving

I'm grateful for the breath in my lungs
I'm thankful for good morning hugs
I'm grateful for my community of family and friends
I'm thankful for God's love that never ends
I'm grateful for a roof over my head
And a comfy, cozy, nice warm bed.
I'm grateful that I have food on my plate
I'm even thankful when I have to wait.
I'm grateful for the clothes on my back
But if I'm being honest sometimes I'm like an amnesiac
Because I forget to count the blessings that I'm grateful for
And sometimes I lose sight of what I have been given and ask for more
But the Lord is good, generous and kind

And brings each one back to my mind
I cannot begin to fathom the many ways
So I sing Him a song of thanks and praise
He has been so good to me
Even working in ways that I cannot see
I'm sure I'm not the only one to be blessed beyond measure
So to you I say cherish each blessing as you would a treasure
Make Thanksgiving more than one day long
Let it be a way of life — a beautiful song
Emanating from your heart to your lips
Gratitude rising to the Giver of every perfect gift.
Today I thank the Lord for all He has given
And most importantly for His unending love and provision.

Hannah Gonneville

By Ray Whitaker
Username: whitjr

Morning Exercises

I write to the world this day
to sense the wonder
asking it to remember the chances
of its beauty.

In writing to the world this day
it is the joy of simply Being
of participating with your God
in bringing the depth of a springtime thaw.

The snowmelt engorges the stream
a long male member pushing down

the meadow below awakens with it

there is a newness to the banks
with the stimulated green
coming from deposits of a fertile brown, fine alluvium

beavers repair their woven dams
spreading water over stream banks
the long winter's nights have given work to them
see them smile as they cut new limbs to weave

the farmer looks back on the newly plowed field
satisfied that the new shoots
will raise their green heads
towards the sun.

The poets write to give
a sense of the wonders
the beauty of broken winter
the people rely on us to do so
to remind them that their paths
aren't necessarily muddy.

If even for only a few moments
the readers and listeners to the words
that even the mighty oaks
grow new leaves to shade us.

II

Forget what justifications as there may be

giving a elusive credence
to the crimes against humanity
the narcissistic despots propagate

the killing
the dying
an unnatural cycle created by constructs
of pursuing wealth above the spirit.

Stepping over the pollution
of plastic washed up on our ocean shores
ignoring the warning barks of our dog brothers
telling us to beware

we are all animals, children on our solid continents
unheard are the cries
from a wounded Mother Earth
that is rebelling against the wounding.

It is the lance from the picadors
bleeding red drops to the arena ground.

III

I write to the world this day
to again feel warm wonder
asking it to bring forth the new growth
of its beauty.

In writing to the world this day
to the joy of simply Being in tune
with your God's sent purpose
in bringing growth to this spring's thaw

touch the sprouts emerging
see the little yellow birds
on the tree limbs happily in the white flowers there
feel the smiling warmth of your dog brother

have seeds of wonder grow
in your place, from the ground of what is possible.

We poets write to give away strength
sourcing the pictures of their universal wonders
the people rely on us to do so
showing the beauty in the winter breaking
to remind them that their paths
aren't necessarily rocky

focus on what color your beauty is
and that warmth from a bright and gentle sun.

Ray Whitaker

By Vicky Rosas
Username: vickyc24

Grateful For The Moments

Life can be wonderful in moments full of joy.
In the moments where you experience a sense of extreme gratitude because of how blissful it feels.
In the moments when your surroundings take your breath away.
In the moments you whisper underneath your breath, "I don't want this to ever end."
In the moments you want to replay in your mind repeatedly.
Yet, in the moments of turmoil, you want to fast forward to the ending.
In the moments of experiencing the chaos, I learned to claim my emotions.
In the moments that the pain felt infinite, I learned to show myself more grace.

In the moments I felt alone and confused, I was led to rediscover myself.
In the moments of hardship, I was taught to persevere.
I am grateful for all the moments that this life has to offer.

Vicky Rosas

By Rick Writes
Username: rickwrites

Faithful, Thankful, Grateful

I am grateful For:

My sons laugh, where his eyes close and he reveals a smile that heals every wound that's ever been afflicted,

For the woman who has always been in my corner even when I was circling my darkest days,

For the abundance of energy that I curate and the way my attitude has shifted,

For my parents who worked hard and showed me the old ways,

For the fortitude I've been afforded when my troubles were consistent,

For the metal rods holding me together and there was no co pay,

For my friends that heard my poetry and made me perform, they insisted,

For my fellow vets who checked on me when they knew I wasn't ok,

For the love I now give my body and the openness to holistics,

For me living with love and not having room for no hate,

For all my friends that deployed who were never injured by ballistics,

For the opportunity to switch schools that I took back in 08,

For the work ethic instilled in me I project with persistence,

For the faith that I won't live forever, but my words will succumb to no date,

For the truth in my tongue that wants to help elevate existence,

No late times in the grand design,

For the great spirit and to my future self I'm so faithful,

I hope I emanate all things I am so grateful.

Rick Writes

By Rashan Speller
Username: artistphilly

Elder Stars In The Star

In the moment I share the stage with you, a man amongst the ruins of personality and beauty. Your words inspire me, the qualities of a man that I climb the ladders of ancestry and slowly achieve this image you see. A brave man who stepped into his skin, exhibiting scars of times when processing your riddles of masculinity was a mystery. A formidable opponent where it would take decades of pruning for me to finally grow a sturdy garden of belief. And yet you carried me a seed to term and watered me with wisdom and love In the soils where nothing returns. I'm grateful for you graduating in your class of life. My gratitude shakes the core of my soul. You leave me in physical shock and ache for your eyes closed to the stars of cancer as they pinch the life away from you into the emotional seas of heaven.

Shine bright star of stars, and shine bright your dreams into mine. So elder star in the sky reuniting the DNA inside. Collect the God in you and rain down the ideal of your life.

Rashan Speller

By Oswald Perez
Username: opwriter

On My Own Two Feet

Dear, Unsealers:

I'm grateful to be on my own feet. Each day, I see them with all the scars and calluses as symbols of confronting the biggest struggle with having cerebral palsy.

Yet, they've carried me from the streets of NYC to sailing around the islands of Santorini. They wobble and tire out easily but they don't give up on enjoying life.

It's with that idea in mind that this poem came along:

I'm grateful for being on my own two feet

Unseal Your Gratitude

As I'm able to open my eyes
And see them in scarred, callused glory

It wasn't always this way, though...

Years of being held back
By varying braces and orthopedics
A mentality that sunk into my mind

Of being helpless
When all I wanted to do was walk
With normalcy, like everyone else

Now, I treasure each step
Whether it's out of my room, walking down the block or in a new destination

No matter the difficulty
On hills, boats and all uneven terrain
I step into my power

To be on my own two feet
A feeling that's worth so much to me

Gratitude doesn't do it enough justice
For the magic of walking on my own two feet

Oswald Perez

By Sydney Stablein
Username: sstablein

Reverence

Gratitude is without attitude
No matter the altitude your life persists
No matter the will your soul must lift
The struggles come with bliss
Don't you see young miss?
Be grateful for the air you breathe
And all the opportunities thus missed
For life would take you down a course of flames and grit
A journey of ease is a journey of a wimp
For I am a warrior and will always persist

The game of life comes with twists
Some of those will make you lose your wit
For I am keen on knowing the end

But what is the fun in future pretense?
Shed your worries like it is skin
And you shall see it's all in your head
I am grateful for the life I've lived
For it has made me whole and intense
I wouldn't be the me I am today
The me I love and the me that prays
Thank you Source for all the lessons
And in return I give you reverence

Syd the Wiz

By Latasha T. Collins
Username: latashatc

I Am Grateful

I am Grateful

I am grateful for the sight to see.
I am grateful for the life inside of me.
I am grateful for the heavens and the sea.
I am grateful for the ground I walk on beneath my feet.
I am grateful for all the birds and the trees.
I am grateful for the unconditional love that God gives me.
I am grateful for the fact that I can breathe.

I am grateful for my son and all my family.
I am grateful for the wonderful
friends that I have around me.
I am grateful for all the things I have and need.

I am grateful for the blood that I bleed.
I am grateful for helping people that have less than me.

I am grateful for my heart that
beats inside of me.
I am grateful for the Earth and the universe.
I am grateful for all my blessings.
The ones that are seen.
The ones that are unseen.
I am grateful for everything.
I am grateful for the blood of
Christ that washes me clean.

Latasha T. Collins

By Kebe Chet
Username: kebe_chet

Gratitude

Hurt doesn't scare me
It only brings clarity
Misery I can't condone
It's all love in my home
Is it a problem this pain's become addicting?
Im either insane or a willing victim
As long as I can feel 1 thing
Because emptiness is crushing
& when I'm not in my body
It's really something to feel your touching
Seems to me
They can't see what I see
On the precipice of all that I can be
& every me I ever was

Being just because
How you gonna shame me into greatness?
It's innate so nothing can take it away
Not even me
For that I am eternally grateful.

Tasia

By Obincent Cineus
Username: bincent24gmailcom

Opportunity And Change Harmonizing With Attitude Of Gratitude

The commencement can be formidable, but conquering fear, and letting reason prevail sets in motion a surge of untapped capabilities.

Become intentional of the route for what you desire and destined to be. What will master over your course or your final fate. Is it fame, love, or fortunes knocking at your door steps? Are you going to answer to any or crumble in your indecisiveness to live a life of regrets and drown in sorrow.

Time does not discriminate and awaits no souls or foes. An attitude of gratitude is a priceless commodity that tends to be the light at the end of the tunnel in our darkest hours which restricts our dreams from imploding and rather exploding into a masterpiece.

Yet so intricate but so fragile is the anticipation and anxiety with father time and uncertainties of mother nature with the inevitable escape of death creeping with every season and changes we make for history not to repeat itself not to seek vanity or lose morality to condemn failure and uselessly implore. Would you rather not want more?

You are the author of your life
Take your stride and strife to fight
Feel the burning torrent rage in your bones
Stand up to fury and flip the page because yesterday's worries are no longer a part of today's story.

As the sun lays to rest and the moon awakened from its slumber it showcased that tomorrow brings another opportunity and changes that you can not hide. Muster up the strength of a mustard seed and reveal your resilience to conquer and overcome any obstacles obstructing your reach of your endeavors.

For that constant breath flowing through your nostrils is the sole purpose of an attitude of gratitude that change is always presented with an opportunity for self betterment.

Obincent Cineus

By Karissa Howden
Username: karissahowden

Simple Gratitude

It's being home for bedtime
And adequate sleep too.
Slow down activities —
long walks, sipping coffee, stretching,
just to name a few.
Fresh baked bread more often than not
Me? Who would've ever thought.
Every day I change,
Old me would think it's so strange.
We're not chasing the money or the beers
Just staying aligned despite any fears.
Success to me looks different now —
I'm grateful for those long, difficult, learning years.

Karissa Howden

By Maria Colon-Gonzalez
Username: shinemdwrites

Transformation

I am grateful for the tears.
I am grateful for the laughter.
You wounded my spirit, but in the end, I am so much stronger.
Your ignorance sucked the life out of me, but I found a new friend that breathed life back into me.
I made a new friend, she is awesome!
It's awesome to have you here with me!
You are wise and strong. You are a friend who pushes me to persevere when all seems like dying. Wake up, my friend, you whisper.
With you by my side, tasks become a breeze, and my day becomes more manageable. You whisper, keep walking; you are smiling.
The backpack is light for you; incredibly, you are my friend.

Please stay with me and continue to teach me to fly like a feather.

I made a new friend!

After many tears, heart racing, and a wounded spirit, I could let go.

It was all thanks to you, my new friend! You gave me the strength to keep going. You whispered, stay alive, wake up, work, and rest. You helped my heart breathe again. I am grateful, my friend.

I am glad you came alive; I am so happy you are my new friend.

My new friend does not seek justice; she surrenders to the destiny of the World. After all, what is justice when the wound took who I was?

Perhaps Justice is my new friend. Maybe justice is rising.

My new friend is trustworthy. I learned your instincts are correct and will always protect me.

I am grateful for my new friend. Without the many tears, maybe I would have never met you.

I am grateful I have a new friend. My friend is firm in boundaries. My friend has no fear of consequences. Bold and audacious!

My friend taught me peace is letting go. Detaching, I can breathe.

My friend came with tears, much more than laughter.

You wounded my spirit, but I have a new friend.

Arise, my friend; your smile and eyes bring life to my eyes.

I let go, I detach, you no longer inflict pain.

Now, my friend and I are working, achieving, dreaming, and thriving.
You do not have the power.
I have a new friend. You no longer have me.
I have a new friend.
Tonight I drink! Here's to many more unique experiences together on our journey! Please don't go, my friend!
Thank you for being here! Tonight, I drink to the tears.
You were there with me. As tears flooded me, you came; you saved me from myself.
Slowly, you were born deep from inside of me.
Then you whispered, Your help is always near! Wake up, my friend!
I saw your smile.
I have a new friend.
Her fairness is admirable.
Her safety is reliable.
I am grateful you are my friend.
You make my life full of brilliance, hope has arisen, you are my friend.
Thank you for being here.
I am grateful, I say.
May the pain and tears come; maybe I will find a new friend.
You whisper, no pain; it is all transformation.
No challenges. It is all transformation.
No learning. It is all transformation.
No resiliency, but growth and transformation.
You live inside me; I have a new friend.

You, my friend, know the secret of transformation.
You arrived at my heart.
Please stay, but you say no, my friend. The time is near.
You know there will be a time of death for you;
transformation is near again. A new friend is arriving.
I am thankful for you, my friend.

Dr. M

By Vision
Username: vizo2123

Mi Beautiful Musician

The moment I locked my eyes on yours
It felt like magic
An instant connection
All we did was smile at one another
We knew what it was
It was
Love at first sight
For the first time in my life
I felt a feeling I Haven't felt before
It's not the same old saying
Oh I Like her cause she's different from the rest
No
It's a feeling where my heart beats a million beats a minute
It's pounding out my chest to the

Sound of your voice
By the way you look at me
Your intellectual mind
Your touching soul
Your glowing smile
How big you heart is
Mi amor I truly am thankful for you
And all you do
You show me you love me
That you care
You have my heart
I wish to not part
To this special woman I love
I've fallen in love
You make my life worthwhile
You take my away from my reality
Only you are not a dream my love
You are real and true
I get lost in you
I never thought it was gonna be like this
Such a bliss
You amaze me
This is true
Baby soon you'll know it's true
How grateful I am for you
I'll express how I Feel
To show you what I Feel is real

Vision W.

By Zalma

Grateful

It's easy — isn't it
To look back on our life & remember all the worst
All the worst times of our life that always seem to come first
Like the first time — I experienced racism
The first time — I experienced bullying
The first time — my love was used against me
Or the first time — my heart was broken
There was a lot of first of "THE WORST"
But likewise — there were many firsts of the best
Like the first time — I got the job I really wanted
Or the first time — I graduated
Or the time I won my first real fight with ease
Or the first time a family member came home from jail surprising me

There's been a lot of good moments
but I seem to have forgotten a lot of them
I'm doing my best now — to live in the present moment
—To soak it all in
Cause I know there is so much to be grateful for
—There's always been
Like my mom choosing peace & safety over toxicity — for her children
No matter what — she never let fear stop her
She was unbelievable
She was unstoppable
She did the best she could with the hand she was dealt
Like getting that job that not only paid the bills
but also provided us with a warm free house
Or that one time she pointed out to her lawyer — how she was wrong
That was only one of the many steps she took — to obtain our freedom
I still remember the first time she met my little boyfriend
She offered to give us some money
—then suggested we go to Barnes & Noble
to drink some coffee
At the time it was so embarrassing—
But looking back now— She's so funny
We were like 14 — Not 40
I still remember — I tried to avoid repeating history
but somehow history didn't escape me
One day — I had to text my mom discreetly

I asked her to please come save me
I won't go into detail — but that day she rescued me from hell
I remember the times my brother and I would go skating
Or when he'd take me to school in his little Honda
Hatchback — I'd say we made some good memories
While others were bittersweet
I wish I could remember them all
but disassociation got the best of me
So here's a few more that easily come to mind
Like when my first love never made me feel pressured
— Simply loved
Or when my second one spoke a prayer over me
That felt majestic & empowering
— Like freedom
Or when my friends and I thought we were cute — walking around the east side
Just waiting on the cute boys to drive by and say hi
Haha — those sure were the good times.
Then there was that time an important figure in my life somehow ended up in jail
Managed to post bail & still make it back in time to my baby shower
Or when that amazing teacher who quickly became family
Went out of her way to pick me up for school daily
Or when another amazing teacher who often went above and beyond
Was touched by some writing assignment I did
& surprised me with an unexpected gift
So yeah —

It is easy to remember all the worst — but there is also so much to be grateful for
I'm grateful for every glimpse of heaven I've ever received
I'm grateful for a badass mom & her vision to always
Push forward & succeed
I'm grateful for the village that helped raise me
I'm grateful for any friend who served a purpose in my life
Even if at some point — our lives no longer aligned
I'm still grateful for the good times & the memories left behind
I'm grateful for the short-lived respect & pure love I received
— from my first love
My impossible baby
I'm grateful for the amazing son — my second one gave me
There is so much more to be grateful for
even from all the worst that were followed by the best
Or I don't know — maybe fue al revés
Either way — I thank you God — My best friend
May I always be able to shine the light on the better side of perspective
May I continue to be able to see all the good that still lives within the broken world we currently live in
May we not only see the trauma we've endured through our struggling
But the perseverance & resilience we received simultaneously
So for both the good & the bad
I gotta be grateful for it all — and I am

Zalma

By Anita Williams
Username: chynell1

A Truth To Return To

I can hear the thunder brewing in the distance, miles away.
I can see the sun's rays beaming through the clouds.
I can feel the wind brushing gently past my skin.
I can taste the unique aroma of my morning tea blend.
I can smell the baked goods at the local cafe down the street.
How romantic is it all?
To hear nature,
to smell it,
to taste it,
to see and feel it,
and to then realize that we are all one and not separate
from it.
Returning to this truth fills each fragment of my heart
with gratitude.

Anita Williams

By Michelle Julian
Username: michellejulian

To My Ancestory

The answers are there, my story is written
One heart shared, no pieces missing.
The fate of our lives conquered and bartered.
Promiscuous past lives stacked on each other.
I stand here on my ancestors' backs,
fogged with bewildering dreams, I hoped to build anew.
How did I impress you? Have you helped me see clearly?
Has your ghost propelled me forward when I was trapped in the dark?
The stories I knew, were possibly mixed. Painted in red but bottled in blue.
The vision of power is momentary bliss, the bliss of power that once lit up the past.
She once felt the life I have.

Did she dream the same as me
although our outlooks and battles were unmatched?
Did we learn the same lessons, chewed up and spit back?
The lowest days of my life I dreamed of you.
The image sparked a fire within me filled with gratitude.
The answers are there, in front of my eyes,
written in my palms, and spoken from my mind.
It is clear as day if I let it be.
I dare see,
how the past created me.

Michelle Julian

By Ricardo Albertorio
Username: gorilladna

Gratitude

What doesn't kill me

Makes me stronger

So I can live

A little longer

To hold you through

Hot summer nights

And then enjoy

Those winter lights

'Cause days go by

So very fast

But slowing down

Can make time last

Your smile, your breath

Your touch, your kiss

To be with you

Is all I wish

And when we're old

And weak and frail

I want the world

To speak our tale

Of love and hope

And fortitude

Of living life

In gratitude

Ricardo Albertorio

By Mel Taul
Username: itsedible

D. All Of The Above

My arms; they're scrunched up to my sides as I thumb my way through this thought. We sleep in one big bed now. Our bed, we call it. As it turns out, sleepovers aren't just for when you have company.

It's a feeling.
It's a spot.
It was a time.
It's yet to come.
It's in my daydreams.
It's in my breath — coming in and out of my lungs.
It lives in a poem my heart rewrites every trip around the sun.
It lives at my grandmother's kitchen table and in the hourly sounds her clock made.

Sometimes it's my feet in the dirt.
Others it's in low lighting, having tea with a friend.
It finds me when I'm well.
It guides me when I'm unwell.
It's what I didn't know I needed.
It's what I don't know how to ask for.
It is peace, when I've surrendered.
It is joy, after sorrow.
It is laughter, while I'm crying.
It is closing my eyes, then getting to open them again.

It is in the seasons.
Coming with the sun rising in the East
And going with the sun setting in the West.
It is fleeting.
It is ever so slow.
It is all of the seasons bound together.
It is my life.

That's it!
I found it.
What am I most grateful for?
My life.
Their lives.
Your life.
All bound together —
All of our experiences.
It's in the mundane.
It burrows itself in my sorrow, just to bloom again with time.

It is my fear unmasked.
It is the ebb and flow.
It's every year wiser.
It is slowing down, just to speed up.
It's in my friendships.
My jobs.
My family.
My passions.
My failures.
My pain.
It is worth all of it, all over again just to feel it again.
It is in who I was when I entered this world.
It is in who I am tucked into our family bed writing this poem.
It is me, alive.

It is D.) All of the above

Mel Taul

279

280

If you would like to read more stories or write your own, head to TheUnsealed.com

Acknowledgments

Thank you to all our contributing writers who have bravely shared their truth to help change the world. One story, one poem, at a time, you all are making a difference. Thank you!

About The Unsealed Founder, Lauren Brill

Lauren Brill is a seven-time Emmy-nominated and AP-award-winning journalist. Throughout her tenure as a television broadcaster, she worked as a sports anchor and reporter for the ABC affiliate in Cleveland, the CBS affiliate in Buffalo and MSG Varsity in the New York metropolitan area. Also, she has written features for several nationally known outlets, including NBA.com, WNBA.com, NikeWomen.com, ESPN's Girl Mag and womensprosoccer.com.

In 2019, she combined her skills as a writer and television journalist to create The Unsealed. She ghostwrites The Unsealed's featured letters, provides commentaries and hosts a weekly interactive show called Unsealed Conversations. People Magazine, ESPN, ABC, The New York Post and E! Online are among the outlets that have acknowledged The Unsealed's work.

At Columbia University, Lauren majored in sociology, focusing her studies on the impact of sports on society.

Made in the USA
Middletown, DE
09 April 2024

52661355R00170